ISBN: 978129037855

Published by:
HardPress Publishing
8345 NW 66TH ST #2561
MIAMI FL 33166-2626

Email: info@hardpress.net
Web: http://www.hardpress.net

THE LIFE

OF

ST. JULIANA OF CORNILLON.

S. Julianna of Cornillon.

THE LIFE

OF

ST. JULIANA OF CORNILLON.

BY

GEORGE AMBROSE BRADBURY, O.C.,

MOUNT ST. BERNARD'S ABBEY, LEICESTERSHIRE.

" Confiteor tibi Pater, Domine cœli et terræ, quod abscondisti hæc a
sapientibus et prudentibus et revelasti ea parvulis."

" I confess to Thee, O Father, Lord of heaven and earth, because Thou
hast hidden these things from the wise and prudent, and hast
revealed them to little ones."—St. Luke, x. 21.

𝔓𝔢𝔯𝔪𝔦𝔰𝔰𝔲 𝔖𝔲𝔭𝔢𝔯𝔦𝔬𝔯𝔲𝔪.

LONDON:
THOMAS RICHARDSON AND SON;
DUBLIN, AND DERBY.
NEW YORK: HENRY H. RICHARDSON AND CO.
MDCCCLXXIII.

TO

MARY IMMACULATE,

THE

PATRONESS OF THE CISTERCIAN ORDER,

THIS

LIFE OF ST. JULIANA

IS DEDICATED,

BY THE

MOST UNWORTHY OF HER CHILDREN.

PREFACE.

"God's ways are not as our ways, neither are His thoughts as our thoughts." What the world despises and casts aside as worthless, that He often uses as an instrument for the accomplishment of His greatest works. There are many examples which prove this.

When He had determined to deliver the children of Israel from Egyptian bondage, not Aaron who was eloquent, but Moses who was slow of speech, was chosen to be the leader of His people. When Goliath defied the hosts of Israel, God did not choose any of Saul's warriors, men of might, men of renown, to fight against this uncircumcised Philistine, but

He took David from the sheepfold, and giving him no other arms than a sling and a few stones; with these simple weapons God gave him the victory over the enemy of His chosen people Israel.

So again, when the fulness of time was come, and God sent forth His Son to redeem the fallen world, the Eternal Word did not choose her who was to be His Blessed Mother from among any of the great ones of this world, but made choice of Mary, the humble, lowly, but thrice Blessed Virgin of Nazareth. Again, when the Gospel of Jesus Christ was to be preached throughout the world, our Lord did not choose for His messengers the great, the learned, the worldly wise; but made choice of poor, ignorant, despised, illiterate fishermen, and gave to their words such power, authority, and unction, that in a short time the name of Jesus was known from end to end of the world.

Thus are the maxims and principles of worldlings altogether different from those of God. The world values nothing, esteems nothing, but riches, power, wealth, and what it is pleased to call greatness and magnificence; these it makes use of in every undertaking: but God most frequently chooses the weak things of this world to overcome the strong, and the foolish things of this world to confound the wise.

The Life of St. Juliana presents us with another example of this mode of God's dealing with His creatures. When He had determined to establish in His Church a Feast in honour of the most Blessed Sacrament of the Altar, He did not choose any prince or potentate to be the first to declare His Will, but made choice of a poor, humble, obscure, almost unknown nun, to manifest His designs.

Yes, it was to the Blessed Juliana that God first revealed His designs, relative to the institution in Christ's Church of the Feast of Corpus Christi.

Her life and actions have been written

by various Latin and other authors. The present is an attempt, although a very poor and imperfect one, to present her Life to English readers. Poor as it is, however, I believe that it has at least the merit of being the first Life ever published in English of the Saint, to whom, under God, we owe the Institution of that Feast of triumph, that Feast which gladdens all Catholic hearts, the Feast of Corpus Christi.

The facts connected with the life of St. Juliana, which are related in this small history of her actions, have been taken from most authentic sources, and nothing has been here related of her, which has not already been many times asserted by authors whose veracity no one can call in question.

May God in His mercy grant that this little book may enkindle in the hearts of all its readers devotion to this sweet Saint, who had such a tender and affectionate devotion to the Sacrament of Love, the

Eucharist. Above all, may He grant them the grace to imitate her in this devotion. If it should have this effect, I beg all who read it to pray most fervently and earnestly for the conversion of our beloved country, so that by their fervent prayers they may obtain from the Bountiful Giver of all good things that, once again, even in England, (which has been so long wrapt in the darkness of heresy,) Jesus may be loved, blessed, praised, and adored by all in the Sacrament of His Love. Moreover, I also beg, that they will not forget the author in their prayers before the tabernacle where Jesus dwells.

BROTHER AMBROSE BRADBURY.

Abbey of our Lady of Mount St. Bernard,
Leicestershire.
Fifth Sunday after Easter, 1872.

CONTENTS.

THE LIFE

OF

ST. JULIANA OF CORNILLON.

THE LIFE

OF

ST. JULIANA OF CORNILLON.

CHAPTER I.

THE BIRTH AND CHILDHOOD OF THE BLESSED JULIANA.

St. Juliana, commonly called St. Juliana of Cornillon, (this being the name of the convent of which she was afterwards prioress), was born at a village called Retine, about six miles from Liége, in Belgium, in the year of our Lord, 1193.

Her father's name was Henry, and her mother's Frescinde. According to some authors, they were of noble extraction, others say that they possessed little of this world's goods. This however matters little, since, in the eyes of God, virtue and sanctity are far more pleasing than any temporal advantages of birth or station.

Henry and Frescinde had been many years married, and God as yet had given them no children. This was a source of great trouble to them, and they ceased not to implore God to be gracious to them, and render their union fruitful.

1

To obtain this favour they gave alms, practised all
kinds of good works, and continually poured out
their hearts before the Lord, praying, weeping,
and begging Him to grant them their desire.   At
length He heard their cry, and gave them a
daughter, whom they called Agnes.   Since very
little will be said of her in this history, it may be
as well to mention here, that all writers agree that
she lived an innocent and holy life, but scarcely
any give the date of her death.   She entered the
convent of Cornillon with her sister, the Blessed
Juliana.   Father Chrysostom Henriquez mentions
her in his "Menologium Cistertiense," and
states that she was buried at Salsines, near
Namur; he then adds this eulogium, "Having
attained a high degree of sanctity, she, after passing through many labours and tribulations, hath
obtained eternal rest."*

The year following the birth of Agnes, our
saint was born.   Her parents had certainly no
reason to hope for this second daughter, since
they were already advanced in age.   They did not
neglect to return thanks to God for having so
graciously listened to their petitions.   It was not
however, His blessed will that they should long
enjoy this blessing.   Henry and Frescinde both
died when our Juliana was only five years old.

Fortunately, however, the guardians of Agnes
and Juliana were fully aware of the importance of
giving to the poor orphans a truly Christian education ; to secure this, they placed them in a
religious house, where they could learn from their
infancy the maxims and truths of the Gospel, and
where every opportunity would be afforded them of
acquiring the science of the saints.

Agnes and Juliana were therefore placed in the

* Men. Cist., Jan. 21, p. 23.

convent of Cornillon, belonging (at the time our saint entered) to the Cistercian Order. From the fact of this house, *after* the Blessed Juliana was compelled to abandon it, having been given to the Augustinians, some have supposed that the house belonged to this Order at the time that Juliana was prioress. But most authors seem to consider her being a Cistercian a fact so well known, that to dispute about it would only be waste of time. Father Chrysostom Henriquez, in his "Menologium Cistertiense," several times mentions the house of Cornillon. Now his authority as a Cistercian historian is certainly very great; he is quoted as perfectly worthy of credit by several authors, among others the celebrated Görres in his "Mystic," frequently quotes him. Henriquez says, "The house (Cornillon) is outside the city of Liége; of old it belonged to our Order, (the Cistercian), but after the departure and death of the Blessed Juliana, the Cistercian Brothers and Sisters, (there were two houses, one of men and the other of women, as we shall see farther on,) being thrust out, others were introduced, who lived under the rule of St. Augustine, and who had the care of the lepers, and they remain there until this day." "Domus Corneliensis est ad portas Leodienses, olim nostri instituti, sed, exclusis post beata Julianæ discessum, et obitum Cistertiensibus Sororibus et Fratribus, qui leprosorum curam habebant, Sorores aliæ ad normam B. Augustini viventes introductæ sunt, quæ usque in hodiernum diem ibidem perseverant."*

Again, speaking of Sapientia, who was the instructress of Blessed Juliana, and afterwards prioress of Cornillon, he says: "She was happy,

---

* Men. Cist. p. 3.

because, being taken from this calamitous life,
she obtained eternal felicity; before that the
house of Cornillon, which she then saw flourish-
ing under the Cistercian rule, was broken up, and
our sisters having been expelled, others of another
institute obtained the place." " Felix verò, quia
ex hac ærumnosa vita subtracta, ad æternam
felicitatem conscendit, antè quàm Corneliensis
Domus, quam ipsa sub Cistertiensi instituto flo-
rentem conspexerat, destrueretur, et expulsis
Sororibus nostris, aliæ alterius instituti locum
obtinerent."*   Again, speaking of the Blessed
Juliana, the same author says : " Besides a certain and constant tradition, which declares her to
have been a Cistercian, it is also the common
opinion of almost all authors.   Now, although
some make no mention of our Order when they
write her life, by no means do they assert that
she did not belong to it.   There are, on the
contrary, many who declare her to have lived
under our institute, but hitherto no one has
denied it."†   So that it is evident in the time of
Henriquez, (he wrote in 1627,) the Blessed
Juliana was universally believed to belong to the
Cistercian Order.   Moreover, we find that whenever, through the persecutions of her enemies, she
was compelled to leave her house, (and this happened several times, as we shall see,) she always
fled for refuge to the Cistercians, which she certainly would not have done, if she had not belonged to that illustrious Order.   Finally, a
plenary indulgence is upon her feast granted to
all the Brethren and Sisters of the Cistercian
Order, belonging to the Reform of La Trappe,
and this indulgence is thus annually marked in
the "Ordo de la Trappe :" " Indulgence plénière.

* Men. Cist. p. 104.   † Men. Cist. p. 109.

Ste. Julienne, Vierge de notre Ordre." "Plenary Indulgence. St. Juliana, Virgin, of our Order." This certainly seems conclusive, and after this we cannot be blamed for asserting that the Blessed Juliana belonged to the Cistercian Order.

Agnes and Juliana being too young to be received amongst the religious, were placed in one of the farm houses belonging to the convent, and the prioress confided the care of their education to a religious of great virtue and sanctity, whose name was Sapientia. She endeavoured by all means to gain the affections of the children committed to her charge, and as Agnes and Juliana were naturally docile and affectionate, she succeeded admirably. This she did in order the more easily to draw them to God, for she well knew, that if she desired her pupils to follow her instructions, it would be of the utmost importance to show them that she really cared for and loved them. They quickly learned to read, and Sapientia taught them the first elements of Christian doctrine. But while neglecting nothing that could contribute to their advancement in learning, she was most of all assiduous in exhorting them to the practice of every virtue. She frequently spoke to them of the nothingness of the things of this world, of the ineffable, never-ending, and unspeakable joys of heaven, which are the reward of all those who have loved and served God in this world. At other times she would speak to them of the torments of hell, and their eternal duration, telling them that this was the inevitable portion of the wicked and of those who forget God. She also often spoke to them of the immense love God has for His creatures, how He has manifested this love in our creation and redemption; then she would impress upon them the duty of returning love for love, and would conclude by begging them to give their young hearts entirely to this God of love. She inspired them with the greatest horror, not only of mortal sin, but even of the slightest fault, painting in the most vivid colours the fatal consequences which sin never fails to bring upon those who give themselves up to its seducing pleasures. She also warned them of the danger of leading a tepid life, telling them how in this state we by little and little give up the practice of good works, and become indifferent about the things of God and our soul's salvation. She often took them to the church and to the convent, telling them to take particular notice of all they saw there. Upon their return she would recall to their remembrance the modesty, activity, and piety with which the religious went to prayer, and the fervour with which they persevered in this holy exercise. She then described to them the exercises of the religious life in detail, its labours on the one hand, and its sweet, serene, and heavenly repose on the other. She often told them that there is no state of life in which we can serve our Lord with greater perfection and security than in religion.

Juliana, whom God had endowed with all the beautiful qualities which render children amiable, attractive, and docile, listened with avidity to the instructions of her holy mistress. The seed fell upon good ground, and was even at this early age bringing fruit a hundredfold. It is recorded of her that nothing puerile was ever observed in her; she took no delight in the games and sports which are ordinarily the great delight of children. For although this kind of amusement is not only allowable, but in many cases absolutely necessary, yet we find, in reading the lives of almost all those who have reached a high degree of sanctity, that in their childhood they have abstained from these sports. They seem instinctively to have avoided everything that could in any way disturb that peace and tranquillity with which God had filled their souls. So it was with Juliana, who, as an old chronicler remarks, "Although young in years was old in understanding and spirit," and had already chosen that "better part" which was never to be taken away from her. She was reserved in her words, grave in her manner, modest in her exterior, and an ardent lover of solitude and retreat.

She learned the whole Psalter by heart, and took great delight in constantly repeating and meditating upon these inspired songs of the Royal Psalmist.

Whenever Sapientia related to her any act of heroic virtue, she always strove to imitate it. We will give an example of this. The life of St. Nicolas, Bishop of Myra, having been read to her, she was struck with that part of it in which it is related that when an infant, although on other days he frequently sucked his nurse's milk, yet on Wednesdays and Fridays he only sucked once, and that towards evening; this fast he observed, moreover, all his life. Juliana resolved to imitate him. But she desired to do so in secret: whether through humility, or through the fear of being forbidden, whichever of these it was, she said nothing about it to any one. One day, therefore, that the sisters were fasting, she believed it her duty to fast also; she managed matters so well as to eat nothing all day. But few things could escape the ever vigilant eye of Sapientia, and she by some means or other soon discovered what her young pupil had been doing. Now, in her inmost heart she admired the child's courage, but, fearing that these austerities, practised at so tender an age, would injure her health,

Sapientia appeared very angry, and reprimanded Juliana severely for what she termed her disobedience. "Is it thus," she said, "that you obey me? Have I not told you a thousand times that you must never do your own will, but always consult those who govern you, and conform your will to theirs?"

Juliana, blushing, trembling, confused and ashamed, and imagining that she had committed a great fault, prostrated herself at the feet of Sapientia, and begged pardon in the most humble manner. The mistress, pretending to be very angry, lifted her up, and placed her out of doors in the snow, (for it was the depth of winter), adding, "Since you have so little respect for the orders I give you, remain there and do penance for your sin." Any other child would have wept and cried most bitterly at such treatment: not so Juliana; although the cold was most intense, she remained perfectly calm and tranquil, and the only tears she shed were tears of contrition for the fault of which she believed herself guilty. Sapientia cast frequent glances at her through the window, admiring her, and giving God thanks for having bestowed upon the child the virtue of patience in such an eminent degree. But, fearing to carry matters too far, she said to Juliana: "Rise, go quickly to church and confess your sin." The sweet child obeyed without a murmur. The priest forbade her to do anything in future without the knowledge of her mistress, and as a penance told her to ask for an egg for breakfast. She accomplished her penance just as simply as she had remained in the snow. Sapientia acted in this manner, not out of a spirit of harshness and severity, for she was uniformly kind, affectionate, and indulgent; but she so acted simply to prove the child's humility, patience, and obedience.

Juliana, young as she was, seems to have been fully convinced that if she desired the spiritual fabric to stand, its foundations must be laid in the depths of holy humility. Every time she gazed upon her crucifix, she saw the image of a God Who, to atone for man's pride, took upon Himself the form of a servant, and humbled Himself so far as to die the ignominious death of the cross. At the sight of such astonishing condescension of the God of might and power, she was fully persuaded that no kind of humiliation ought to be repugnant to a Christian. Hence she was resolved to embrace the lowest and most menial offices. She therefore begged most earnestly that Sapientia would confide to her the care of keeping the cows, and cleaning the stables. Sapientia represented to her that these offices would be far beyond her strength, that, being naturally delicate, she would not be able to endure the labours and fatigues of such an employment; that the education that had been given her, rendered her capable of performing duties which would be more honourable, and at the same time less laborious; that she would not be able to endure the offensive smell of the place; and many other arguments of the like kind. But it was all in vain, Juliana still continued to beg that this menial employment might be given her. Sapientia then told her that the desire of obtaining this employment all at once was a mere fit of fervour which would soon pass away; that if she allowed her to exercise these functions, she would quickly be disgusted with them, and would beg as earnestly to be released from them as she now did to be allowed to undertake them. But these representations were equally useless; Juliana, whose desire of obtaining this office, was really an effect of true humility, continued to solicit it, and at last obtained her request.

Full of joy at having at length procured this employment, she went early in the morning to her work, and although the labour became, from time to time, more painful and more disgusting, yet she performed it with so much pleasure and satisfaction, that it was quite evident that to her there was nothing painful, humiliating or repugnant in the discharge of the duties of her state. No one ever heard her complain, or manifest the least distaste or disgust for any of the disagreeable things that happened to her in the performance of her duties. If the beasts threw her upon the ground, or trod her under foot, circumstances of which her sister Agnes has often been an eyewitness, she never complained, and thus by her patience gained much merit. If any little negligence happened to her in the exercise of her multiplied duties, she never failed to accuse herself of it, and do penance for it, and thus practised the virtue of humility.

But it was, above all, in the recollection with which she performed her duties, that her love of God was manifested. While her hands were busily engaged in labour, her heart was closely and intimately united to God, so that she never allowed the activity of Martha to disturb the sweet contemplation of Mary. Hence it was that she quickly learned, that they who exercise themselves in the lowest things, shall speedily be raised to the highest. For, as she thus meditated upon heavenly things, having her heart in heaven, although her hands were employed in the stable, who can tell the mysteries and depths of God's love she discovered in these holy meditations? Who can describe the fire of Divine love they enkindled in her young heart? We can well imagine that God, who is rich and generous to all who invoke Him, did not leave His poor servant without consolation.

She, however, never neglected any of her duties, by reason of this close application of her mind to the things of God. On the contrary, she was most careful to turn everything to the best advantage, having a great desire to benefit the convent temporally as well as spiritually. An old writer assures us that milk, cheese and butter were never so plentiful as when Juliana had the care of the cows. Nor need we be surprised at this; we read in Holy Scripture that when the brethren of Joseph sold him into Egypt, the Lord gave him favour in the sight of his master, and that, moreover, God prospered all his undertakings. Again, when the false representations of his master's wife caused him to be cast into prison, the Lord once more gave him favour in the sight of the keeper of the prison, so that he gave all things into his hands, and the Lord prospered exceedingly all the works of his hands. And when he was delivered out of prison, the Lord so prospered his undertakings, that Pharao called him the saviour of the world.* Now, why did God so prosper Joseph and the work of his hands? Simply because Joseph in all he did had God alone in view. So it was with Juliana; she lived for God alone, and therefore God blessed her labours in an extraordinary manner.

She had a most tender devotion to the Holy Mother of God; in the midst of her labours she would frequently cast herself upon her knees, and with great fervour and devotion recite the Ave Maria. She used also to recite the Canticle Mag-

---

* Gen. xli. 45.

nificat nine times every day, in honour of the nine
months our Lord dwelt in the blessed womb of
Mary. Besides this, she took great delight in
meditating upon the virtues and prerogatives of
this Queen of Virgins. Nor were her meditations
mere dry, cold speculations, but she endeavoured
to put in practice the particular virtue on which
she was meditating. Moreover, she endeavoured
to acquire a great personal love for the ever
Blessed Virgin, well knowing that we cannot
rightly love Jesus, if we do not imitate Him as
far as we can in the immense love He had for His
most Blessed Mother.

Thus did Juliana increase in wisdom and knowledge, and in favour with God and man.

CHAPTER II.

JULIANA ENTERS THE CONVENT OF CORNILLON.

THE Blessed Juliana led this laborious and
obscure life until she was fourteen years of age.
She then begged to be admitted into the society
of the Sisters. The rare virtues of Juliana were
not unknown to the Sisters, for they had ample
opportunity of witnessing her humility, patience
and devotion. They, therefore, most joyfully received Juliana amongst them, thinking that they
should receive great edification from one whose
life hitherto had been more angelic than human.
Nor were they deceived in their expectations.

Juliana, therefore, took the religious habit in
the year 1207, and used every effort to make her
interior dispositions correspond to the exterior

habit. In order that she might the better understand the truths of the Christian religion, she studied the Latin language, in which she made great progress, since, as we shall see further on, having caused a priest to compose an Office of the Blessed Sacrament, she herself undertook its correction. At a time when there were few translations of the Holy Scriptures and Fathers, the knowledge of Latin was a very great advantage. Having once acquired it, she studied the Holy Scriptures, Fathers, and Lives of the Saints with surprising avidity. She stored up in her memory these holy lessons, in order to have recourse to them in time of need. Moreover, she never read or heard of any beautiful feature in the Lives of the Saints, without endeavouring to practise it herself.

Among the writings of the holy Fathers, she took the greatest delight in those of SS. Augustine and Bernard. The burning love with which their hearts were enkindled, being diffused also in their writings, she could not peruse them without her own heart being also inflamed with Divine love. St. Bernard's sermons on the Canticles she read over and over again, with the most intense devotion, nourishing her soul without ceasing, with the sacred unction that breathes in every page. She committed to memory twenty sermons of this holy Father, in order that she might more easily meditate upon them, and she repeated the most beautiful portions of them over and over again with never-failing pleasure. Like a bee which goes from flower to flower to suck the honey from it, so Juliana continued for several years to employ herself in this holy and useful study, extracting all the honey, and laying up a good store of provisions against the day of necessity and tribulation. Thus did this young virgin enter-tain herself with her celestial Spouse, and so by degrees, and as it were insensibly, became disgusted with the things of earth, relishing only those of heaven; and as a reward for her fidelity to Him, the Lord disposed her for a closer and more intimate union with Him.

Juliana's zeal for regular observance knew no bounds; whenever the bell announced any regular exercise, no matter what work she might be engaged in, she immediately discontinued it to obey the signal. She was fully aware that no private devotion or labour is pleasing to God, when performed at the expense of duties prescribed by the rule or holy obedience.

St. Benedict, in his Rule, gives as one sign of vocation in novices, zeal for the Divine Office. Certainly Juliana possessed this in an eminent degree; none were more assiduous in attendance at choir than she, none more fervent in singing the praises of her Divine Spouse. Nothing but sickness, or works of obedience, ever kept her from this holy exercise, and the fervour with which she performed this duty, showed most clearly the love with which her heart was inflamed. The other religious were greatly edified by her profound recollection, her scrupulous attention to all the prescribed ceremonies, and the great fervour which she always manifested for this holy duty.

A heart so full of the love of God, must of necessity be full of love towards its neighbour; consequently, we need not be surprised to find that all the days of Juliana were full days, full of good works. While keeping a constant guard over her heart, never allowing it to give itself to creatures, she always executed with admirable promptitude whatever obedience prescribed. No one ever heard her murmur against, or contradict the orders of superiors; on the contrary, she even frequently anticipated their wishes, or where this could not be done, she, at the slightest intimation, fled to execute their will. Being fully persuaded that in the exercise of charity to her neighbour, she should render herself agreeable to Him who has had so much love for us, she sought every occasion of rendering herself useful to her sisters. If she noticed any whose labours appeared to be beyond their strength, she immediately endeavoured to assist them, no matter how painful or difficult it might be. When the work of any sister, (whether through negligence, sloth, or otherwise,) remained imperfect, she knew how to make up for this deficiency, without its being generally noticed. Nor was this charity extended only to a few; she exercised it towards all indiscriminately, whenever an occasion presented itself. But she always accomplished it with so much wisdom and prudence, that no one was ever offended by it, nor was she ever taxed with acting in this manner, through self-will or vanity. Her manner of acting showed most clearly that she did these things solely from motives of true charity.

A great lover of silence and recollection, the Blessed Juliana avoided with the greatest care all unnecessary conversations with creatures. Her Creator had become the object of all her desires; for Him alone she sighed, Him alone she loved, and all creatures she loved only in Him and for Him. Hence all her leisure moments were spent in entertaining herself with this Supreme object of her love, whether in prayer or in the reading of pious books. Thus did she endeavour to detach herself entirely from things of earth, and cleave only to the things of heaven. If, however, necessity sometimes obliged her to converse with crea-

tures, she always endeavoured to turn these conversations to the greater glory of God; moreover,
she spoke with so much sweetness and charity,
that all who conversed with her were edified beyond measure, and exceedingly admired her
modesty and her ardent love of God. Indeed,
her heart was so full of the love of God, that
when she did speak at all, God's boundless love
for man was always the chief topic of her conversations.

Notwithstanding her many virtues and great
sanctity, she believed herself the last and lowest
of all. Far from attributing anything to herself,
she most firmly believed that she was not corresponding faithfully with the graces God bestowed
upon her. Hence it was that she humbled herself in every possible way, always seeking the
lowest and most menial offices, always content,
and indeed extremely happy, at having the
coarsest and poorest clothing given to her, thinking that, however poor and coarse it might be, it
was still infinitely better than she deserved. In
fine, she was content and happy with everything
that was most vile and abject. And as her humility was sincere and profound, so we are not surprised to find that her obedience was prompt and
perfect, since St. Benedict, in the chapter of his
rule on obedience, says that the first degree of
humility is ready obedience. If this, therefore,
is the *first* degree of humility, we may well believe that it was practised most perfectly by her
who had acquired this virtue, not only in its first,
but also in all its degrees. Nothing was preferred
by her to obedience, not even the sweetness she
felt in prayer: no matter how deeply she might be
plunged in meditation, at the first call of obedience she would immediately leave her devotions,
and go promptly to perform whatever was required

of her. Thus did she in all things renounce her-self. We have seen above how careful the holy virgin was to renounce all exterior objects that could in any way hinder her from the contempla-tion of her Beloved. But she well knew that this is not sufficient; there is a secret and perfidious enemy within, the most dangerous of all, and this enemy is self-love. If man, after having detached himself from all creatures, is still attached to himself, he has done nothing. He has avoided that which appeared to him evil, and remains attached to that which he thinks is good. It is true he is no longer governed by exterior objects ; but he is a slave to himself. It was for this reason that the Blessed Juliana renounced her-self in all things, and walked by the secure path of holy obedience. She said not, "I wish this," or, "I do not wish that," but sincerely endea-voured to go out of herself, without seeking any self-satisfaction. The practice of this self-renouncement gave her every day new strength ; so that being truly free, with the freedom where-with Christ hath made us free, she had her soul in her hands, and gave it to Him who was her Life, her Love, her All. As she sacrificed herself and renounced herself in all things, so did she enjoy that true peace which no adversity could trouble or disturb, because it was the peace which God had given her, as a reward for forsaking all things, the peace of God which passeth all under-standing. God loves nothing in us so much as this perfect self-detachment; hence we need not be surprised that He poured His choicest benedic-tions upon our Saint, who practised it in such great perfection.

Such an amount of virtue in one so young, and a life so edifying, and so conformable to the doctrines and maxims of the Gospel, clearly

2

showed that the Lord had particular designs
upon her, and that it was His will that she should
attain a high degree of sanctity. She, on her
part, endeavoured to fulfil the will of her Spouse,
making continual use of all the instruments of the
spiritual calling, and thus prepared herself to
receive at the day of judgment that reward which
the Apostle St. Paul tells us, " eye hath not
seen, nor ear heard, neither hath it entered into
the heart of man to conceive what things God
hath prepared for them that love Him."*

CHAPTER III.

JULIANA'S LOVE OF PRAYER——HER DEVOTION TO THE BLESSED SACRAMENT.

MAN being once detached from nature and from
self, has accomplished something, but not all, by
any means. It is not sufficient that he no longer
belongs to himself; it is absolutely necessary for
him to belong to God, and to think and act only
in Him. Pride and self-will being once broken,
the superior part of the soul more easily follows
this movement of ascent towards God, and becomes
more capable of a close and intimate union with
Him. But in order that this relation of man
with God may be established, man must earnestly
desire it. Now this desire is manifested in
prayer. " Every prayer," says Rusbroch, " consists in saying to God : O Lord, my God, give me
what You wish, and dispose of me as You please."
It was the prayer of our Lord in Gethsemani :

* 1 Cor. ii. ix.

"Father, not as I will, but as Thou wilt." This
kind of prayer detaches man from nature and the
world around him; it detaches him also from that
little world which is within him ; it purifies him,
and causes him to make an entire sacrifice of all
spirit of self-appropriation. All the saints have
considered prayer, and especially the prayer of
resignation, (if I may so term it), a powerful
means of acquiring a close union with God.
Hence it was that the Blessed Juliana endeavoured to attach herself still closer to God, by
constant and fervent prayer. Blærus tells us that
" all who have written her life, speak of her piety
and zeal for prayer." "We read," he continues,
" that her raptures were frequent, and that she
was endowed with the gift of prophecy, and that
she even penetrated the inmost thoughts of the
hearts of those who came to her for counsel and
advice." She celebrated the feasts consecrated to
the Lord with so much ardour, piety, and devotion, that her sisters regarded her, and with
justice, as the well-beloved spouse of Jesus. The
greater part of the night which preceded the feast,
she passed in prayer and meditation. When, on the
feast of Christmas, she considered her God become
a little Child for love of man, her soul was so
inflamed with Divine love, that, in spirit, taking
the Infant Jesus in her arms, she embraced Him
with unspeakable tenderness and affection of heart.
Then she would contemplate Him lying in the
manger, and would prostrate herself before Him
in profoundest adoration. Again, she would consider Him who gives to all His creatures meat in
due season, Himself deigning to be nourished
with milk from the chaste breast of His holy
Mother, and in these meditations she experienced
indescribable joy. But when she contemplated
Him shedding His blood under the knife of cir-

cumcision, her soul was pierced with the keenest
sorrow, and she would pour forth her most fervent
prayers, begging of Him so to turn the hearts of
men towards Him, that He might never more
be wounded by their sins, crimes, and ingrati-
tude.

As it is in His Passion that our dear Lord has
in a more especial manner shown the immensity
of His love for man, so it was in meditating upon
the sufferings of Jesus in His Passion, that the
heart of the Blessed Juliana was melted away like
wax, and in her meditations a fire was enkindled.
Whenever she applied herself to this meditation,
or that she heard it preached of in the church,
she would shed such an abundance of tears, that
her cheeks, her habit, yea, the very ground upon
which she was kneeling, would be bathed with her
tears. Whenever the hymn, " Vexilla regis
prodeunt," was sung, she was pierced with such
keen and lively sorrow, that she could not prevent
its being observed ; and, in order that she might
not be a distraction to others who were chanting
the office, they were obliged to carry her out of the
church. She knew very well that true sorrow
is in the interior much more than in the exterior ;
but these bursts of sorrow with her were involun-
tary, and proceeded simply and solely from her
vehement love of God, and from the intense grief
she felt at seeing men continually offend Him.
She most ardently desired to be crucified like her
Saviour, and nothing would have given her
greater delight than to have been put to a cruel
and ignominious death for love of Him who died a
most painful death to redeem the world. Since
this could not be accomplished, and that the
crown of martyrdom was not for her, she endeavoured to make up for this as far as she could
by attaching her soul to Him with a love that

knew no bounds. Deeply grieved that she could not perfectly imitate her beloved Jesus, she at least animated herself with courage to bear every kind of pain, labour, and fatigue.

Having so great a love of sufferings, we are not surprised to find that she practised austerities without end; long and painful watchings, labours far beyond her strength, nearly continual fasts, and other macerations, had so reduced her body and exhausted her strength, that her life was, so to say, a continual languor. According to those who lived with her, (and they certainly should be the best judges,) her infirmities were caused by the labours to which she voluntarily subjected herself when she was too young and too weak to bear them, and were not caused by her frequent meditations on the passion, still less from the greatness of the love with which she was inflamed, and which bore her without ceasing towards her God, as to the centre of her beatitude and her eternal repose. On the contrary, this love was her greatest support, and without it she would have infallibly succumbed under the many labours and trials she had afterwards to undergo.

Sapientia, who had lately been elected prioress, had never lost sight of her former pupil; she remarked in her a great devotion to the holy sacrifice of the Mass, and to Jesus in the Blessed Sacrament. She also noticed her great love of solitude, and her extraordinary gift of prayer. After having fully tried by what spirit she was led, and believing that she was led by the Spirit of God, she, in order to second the designs of God upon her, and to give her greater facility for prayer and recollection, caused an oratory to be constructed, in which Juliana could from time to time retire, and give herself up to prayer. Juliana had a long time desired this, but had not dared to request it, lest her own will, instead of the will of her superiors, should be accomplished in the matter. No sooner was it finished than she devoted herself more than ever to a life of solitude and prayer, and it was in this place that she tasted the purest delights of the highest contemplation. Her sisters often found her there rapt in ecstasy, quite motionless, and unmindful of all earthly things, yea, even of her bodily nourishment.

Her sisters, fearing her health would give way if this state of things continued, would beg of her to take some food, and she, out of gratitude to their charity, would do as they desired. But she partook of so small a quantity of food that her life was sustained only by a miracle. Her fasts were so frequent, her abstinence so rigorous, and her complexion and frame so delicate, that unless the hand of God had otherwise supported her, she must have died. Seeking only the spiritual nourishment of the soul, she drew all her strength from her intimate union with her celestial Spouse, preferring, as she herself said, this divine food to all the most exquisite viands the world could produce.

All the feasts that the Church celebrates to honour the mysteries of our holy religion, were for her days of joy and gladness. But she had a most particular affection for the feast of our Lord's Ascension into heaven. Upon this day she was accustomed to go into the garden, and placing herself in the middle of it, she stood, like the apostles of old, " gazing up into heaven." To have seen her, one would have thought that she actually perceived the Saviour triumphing over death and hell, and entering into the possession of His glory. It did indeed seem to her, that she saw Him rise little by little from the earth, and that she heard the harmonious concerts of angels and archangels, of the thrones, dominations and powers, of the cherubim and seraphim, and all the heavenly host, who celebrated with songs of joy the triumphant entry of the Sacred Humanity of our Lord into that heaven which she then seemed to contemplate with the eyes of her soul. It is impossible to describe the torrent of delights which were poured into her soul in these holy contemplations. Upon one of these occasions, a friend of hers, to whom she was accustomed to open her heart, was an eye witness of her devotion. No sooner had Juliana commenced to contemplate the mystery of the Ascension, than she suddenly fell into an ecstasy, and remained immoveable; her companion thought that she was either dead, or was at least expiring, so deeply were the powers of her soul plunged in the contemplation of celestial things. She therefore ran to her assistance, conjuring her by every endearing epithet to make some effort to return to her ordinary state. But it was all in vain, Juliana remained without movement and without speech. It was only after the lapse of some considerable time that she returned to herself, after having uttered, with a deep sigh, the words, "Alas! my God is gone."

Waking up, as if from a deep sleep, and seeing herself deprived of the sight of her celestial Spouse, she was sad and troubled, but was consoled by the remembrance that Jesus is really present, Body, Soul, and Divinity, in the Holy Sacrament of the Altar. At the recollection of this she rejoiced, and continually repeated the divine and consoling promises He has given to us in these words: " Lo, I am with you always, even to the consummation of the world." Then she congratulated herself upon the happiness of really possessing Jesus upon our altars, where she could adore Him with a heart overflowing with love and with transports of joy, more easy to imagine than to describe.

She had also a great devotion for the feasts of our Lady, but of all her feasts, the one she celebrated with most ardent devotion and piety was the feast of the Annunciation. It seemed as if she could never cease from meditating upon and admiring the celestial simplicity of the words of the angel Gabriel; the trouble that his salutation at first gave to Mary, the consent that she gave to become the Mother of God, the profound humility, the more than angelic modesty, and the ardent love, our Blessed Lady displayed upon this occasion. At the thought of the Eternal Word descending from the bosom of His Father, and becoming man for love of us, her heart became so inflamed with love, that it seemed to her she could no longer contain it within her breast.

We have seen that even in her childhood she was very devout to the Blessed Virgin, and she endeavoured also to excite in others still greater devotion for this august Queen of heaven and earth than they already possessed. A devotion that she frequently recommended to the other religious, was to recite the "Ave Maria," and the canticle "Magnificat," nine times every day, in honour of the nine months our Lord dwelt in the womb of His ever Blessed Mother; and she assured them that she was indebted to the practice of this devotion for many favours and graces she had obtained from heaven. Whenever she recited or sung the "Magnificat," she was accustomed to contemplate the fatigues our Blessed Lady suffered in her journey from Nazareth to the house of her cousin Elizabeth. She then considered the tender embraces of those two women so beloved by God, the joy with which St.

John the Baptist leaped in the womb of his
mother, at the approach of Mary, who bore his
Saviour within her womb; then she meditated
upon their holy salutations and the thanksgivings
they afterwards rendered to God.

In fine, we can safely say that the blessed
Juliana most perfectly observed the apostolic precept, "Pray without ceasing." She lived in such
close and continual union with God by prayer,
that even in her sleep she gave utterance to the
most loving ejaculations and amorous sighs for
her Beloved; so that we may say her apparent
sleep was an ecstasy; her repose, a transport of
love; her rest, an occupation full of light and
love: accomplishing those words of the spouse in
the Canticles: "I sleep, but my heart watches."

We have seen that, even in her childhood,
Juliana was a lover of mortification; but this
desire of bringing her body into subjection, "as
the apostle saith," increased with her years. She,
for the last thirty years of her life, fasted every
day, eating only once in the day, and that not
until towards evening; and so small was the
amount of food she took, that it was a marvel how
her life could be sustained. In vain her friends
represented to her that one so frail and delicate
as she was ought to eat at least twice a day, and
that the little nourishment she took was not sufficient to support her; she had become so accustomed to fasting, that she was not able to eat
twice a day even very moderately, and when, to
please her sisters, she endeavoured to do so, her
stomach could not retain the food they gave her.

Several persons who were aware of her feeble
and sickly state, sent her frequently the most
delicate and tempting kinds of food; but the
pleasure they procured her in this, was simply to
give her an opportunity of practising charity, for

as soon as she received these presents she sent
them to the portress, to be given to the poor ; if
she could not have done this, she certainly would
have refused to receive such presents.   The little
sleep that she took was far too short to recruit her
strength ; but she held small account of her
bodily health, her one sole desire was to be united
to her Beloved by the closest possible bonds, and
the better to secure this favour, she gave herself
up to a life of prayer and contemplation.

But of all her devotions, the one which shone
pre-eminently in her, was her extraordinary love
and devotion for the most holy Sacrament of the
Altar.   It is in this Blessed Sacrament that our
beloved Jesus hath, according to the expression
of the sacred Council of Trent, "poured forth all
the riches of His divine love for man."   It is the
sacrament of love, the "love of loves," as St.
Bernard calls it, the strongest pledge of love that
God could give us ; for, as St. Francis of Sales says,
"In no one action can our Blessed Saviour be
considered so loving, so tender, as in this in which
He, as it were, annihilates Himself and reduces
Himself into food, in order to enter into our souls,
and to unite Himself with the hearts of the faithful."   Now, as our Juliana was such an ardent
lover of Jesus, we need not be astonished at her
intense devotion to the thrice blessed Sacrament
in which Jesus hath manifested such infinite love
for poor, weak, helpless, frail, mortal man.   She
was never so happy as when adoring her Beloved
in the Sacrament of the Eucharist, and was so
inflamed with love for her Saviour and God really
present there, that she could never find expressions sufficiently tender, loving, and affectionate,
to declare her gratitude for so great a benefit.
Sometimes she would, in adoring her hidden God,
humble herself, profoundly acknowledging her

utter unworthiness to appear in the presence of
His august Majesty. At other times she would
give vent to the most inflamed expressions of
love. In order to express what she felt and
thought in these moments, we must have been
able to read her heart, and also have been penetrated with her love. Frequent communion was
not the custom of the times in which the Blessed
Juliana lived, otherwise she would have communicated every day, such was her ardent desire to
be fed with the Bread of Angels. But if she
could not do this, she at least communicated as
frequently as she could, without giving occasion to
those around to envy, or tempting them to murmur on account of what would have had the
appearance of great singularity. Upon the days
she did communicate, she avoided as much as
possible all intercourse and conversation with
creatures, entertaining herself with her Creator,
and keeping herself united to Him in the closest
possible manner. Indeed, the joy she felt after
communion was so great and exuberant, that she
could not possibly hide it, whatever efforts she
might make to do so. Her hunger and thirst for
this divine food was so great that she might well
cry out with holy David: "As the hart panteth
after the fountains of water, so my soul panteth
after Thee, O God. My soul hath thirsted after
the strong living God." The more frequently she
communicated, the more did she hunger and
thirst for this celestial Manna, that containeth in
itself all sweetness, and the more ardently did her
heart burn with love for Him, Who, in this heavenly
banquet, hath given Himself for the food and
nourishment of our souls. Her love for this
divine food was so great that it caused her to have
no taste or relish for the things of earth ; united
to Jesus her beloved, her heart became a burning

furnace of love, in which everything terrestrial was entirely consumed. Thinking that possessing her God, she ought no longer to converse with creatures, she entered her oratory, kept a strict silence for eight days, and violated it only for some very pressing and indispensable necessity. The time appeared to her short, so great was the delight she experienced in the celestial entertainments and colloquies she held with her God. What a reproach this is to our tepidity, we who can scarcely spend one quarter of an hour in thanksgiving for the unspeakable benefit our dear Lord bestows upon us when He comes in holy communion to visit our souls.

Her sisters, who really thought that either her health or mind would certainly be injured by such close and intense application to the things of God, endeavoured sometimes to distract her, and represented to her that solitude, her great austerities, and such continual strain upon the mind, would most assuredly lead to the ruin, of her health. But she begged them, with angelic sweetness, to leave her alone with her God for one month, and not to give themselves any concern or trouble about her bodily necessities, since she assured them she no longer had any relish for the bread of earth ; but that the Bread of Heaven contained in itself so much sweetness, suavity and strength, as to make all earthly delights burdensome and disagreeable to her. Only the desire of enjoying God in her retreat, could have caused her to speak thus ; certainly it was not with the intention of passing for a saint, since she looked upon herself as the most imperfect of the whole community.

Whenever she heard the signal for consecration, in whatever place she might be, she prostrated, and repeated the acts of adoration with so much unction and fervour, that it was easy to see her heart was all on fire with love. She heard Mass with so great devotion, that in spite of her humility and the sincere· desire she had to hide her piety, the burning love with which she was interiorly consumed, was exteriorly manifested by her amorous sighs, and by the halo of light which was visible upon her features, and which was sometimes so great as to dazzle the beholders.

Light and darkness, considered under a physical relation, have no moral character ; they are both pure instruments in the hand of Him who hath said by the mouth of the prophet: "I have created light and called darkness." But their opposition can symbolically express the immense difference between good and evil. Thus in the Holy Scriptures heaven is described as a place of light, and hell as a place of darkness. God, in order to shew us the inward beauty of those who are wholly His, His most especial friends, and singularly dear to Him, has frequently caused their countenances to emit rays of light. These luminous phenomena Almighty God has produced in those whom He has elevated to an extraordinary degree of sanctity, innumerable times. It has been manifested in the Old Dispensation as well as in the New. Thus the face of Moses, when he came down from the Mount Sinai, was so resplendent with light that Aaron and the children of Israel were afraid to come near him.* When St. Stephen, the first martyr, stood before the council, his face shone like the face of an angel.† St. Polycarp, a disciple of St. John the Evangelist, and the angel or bishop of Smyrna, who was commended above all the bishops of Asia by Christ Himself in the Apocalypse, and the only one without a reproach, when his executioners set fire to the pile which

* Exod. xxxiv. 29-35.   † Acts vi. 15.

was to have been his martyrdom, the flames, form-
ing themselves into an arch, like the sails of a
ship swelled with the wind, gently encircled the
body of the martyr which stood in the middle, and
which shone with such brightness that its brilliancy could be perceived even through the flames.*
Several times also the martyrs of this time have
been discovered in their dungeons surrounded with
light.   Constantine having sent Photius to pay a
visit to St. Paul the first hermit, and having recommended him to observe well the expression of
his countenance, Photius said to Simeon who
accompanied him, "Although I have often endeavoured to look him in the face, I have never
been able to do so, and have always been compelled to close my eyes, because they were dazzled
by the rays of light which his countenance sent
forth."†

St. Ida of Lewis, of the Cistercian Order, frequently emitted brilliant and splendid rays of
light from her eyes, her face, and sometimes even
from her whole body.‡   Indeed, facts of this kind
sufficient to fill whole volumes might be quoted,
but we have seen enough to be persuaded that this
phenomenon in the Blessed Juliana was the work
of God.   Upon the occasions in which this brightness was seen upon her countenance, she was
generally in ecstasy, and she sometimes became
fixed and immoveable, which shows how intense
her devotion must have been.   The Holy Spirit
had taken possession of her whole soul, had animated her with His breath, and enkindled within
her the fire of His love.   Her faith in the Real
Presence of Jesus in the Sacrament of His love
was so lively, that in His presence she was alto-

* Cir. Let. of Church of Smyrna to the Churches of Pontus.
† Baronius, an. 984.   ‡ Cist. Men. 365.

gether oblivious of earthly things, and mindful
only of the Supreme and only object of her love.
Our Lord on His side poured such an abundance
of light and heat into her soul, that it was even
manifested exteriorly by the brightness of her
countenance; she was in the presence of the
" True Light, which enlighteneth every man that
cometh into the world," and no wonder that she
shone with the light that He imparted to her, and
with which He inundated her soul.

Thus did this blessed soul, when present at the
celebration of the holy mysteries, receive an abundance of grace and strength: she had it bestowed
upon her, because she came prepared to receive
it. She came hungry and thirsty, begging an
alms from Him who is the most generous and
the most bountiful Giver of all good things, and
He, far from sending her away empty, filled her,
on the contrary, with the Bread of Consolation,
and gave her to drink of that living water, which
became in her a fountain springing up into everlasting life. The most blessed privilege to her
(next to receiving Jesus in the Holy Communion,)
was to kneel before the altar of God, there to
adore, love, bless and praise Him for His goodness and mercy to the children of men. She
loved the House of the Lord, and the place where
His Majesty dwelleth, and could well sing with
the holy Psalmist : " How lovely are Thy tabernacles, O Lord of Hosts ! my soul longeth and
fainteth for the courts of the Lord. My heart
and my flesh have rejoiced in the living God.
For the sparrow hath found herself a house, and
the turtle a nest for herself where she may lay her
young ones. Thy altars, O·Lord of Hosts, my
King and my God. Blessed are they that dwell
in Thy house, O Lord : they shall praise Thee for
ever and ever. Blessed is the man whose help is

from Thee : in his heart he hath disposed to
ascend by steps, in the vale of tears, in the place
which he hath set.   For the law-giver shall give a
blessing; they shall go from virtue to virtue : the
God of gods shall be seen in Sion.........Better is
one day in Thy courts above thousands.   I have
chosen to be an abject in the house of my God,
rather than to dwell in the tabernacles of sinners.
For God loveth mercy and truth : the Lord will
give grace and glory.   He will not deprive of good
things them that walk in innocence : O Lord of
Hosts, blessed is the man that trusteth in Thee."*

CHAPTER IV.

JULIANA'S VISION——ITS INTERPRETATION IS REVEALED TO HER.

JULIANA was full of gratitude for the many graces
God bestowed upon her; and as she was deeply
grateful for them, so also did they serve to make
her still more humble ; for she was herself fully
persuaded that if these graces had been granted
to any other, they would have been made better
use of.   She therefore humbled herself before the
Lord, acknowledging her utter unworthiness, and
confessing in presence of His Divine Majesty her
incapability of doing anything good without His
grace and assistance.   Then she would weep over
what she termed her great sins and iniquities, yet
in the eyes of those with whom she lived and
conversed, her life was blameless.   God, who
" resists the proud, and gives His grace to the

* Psalm lxxxiii.   :

humble," was pleased with the humility of His servant, and accordingly rewarded her by bestowing upon her still more abundant graces. He had frequently favoured her before with ecstasy and a close and intimate union with Himself; but now it was His good pleasure to favour her with a vision. He did not, however, upon this occasion, reveal to her its import. One day, therefore, that she was in prayer, she was suddenly rapt into an ecstasy of mind, and beheld a vision in which the figure of the moon was presented before her, shining with great lustre. This moon, however, had one dark spot in it, which took away from it the perfection of its beauty.

Writers do not all agree upon the precise year in which she had this vision; but this by no means destroys the fact of her having had the vision, since discussions of the *dates* of various events are of frequent occurrence, while no one thinks of calling the *events* themselves in question. Thus, while all who have written the life of St. Juliana mention the vision in the same way, they do not all agree as to the year in which it happened. The *fact* is fully and amply authenticated, although the *date* is matter of disputation. The more general opinion, however, seems to be that the blessed Juliana was about sixteen years of age when she received this favour. Juliana, as soon as she returned to herself, was greatly troubled, wondering what the vision could signify, and fearing there might be some illusion, she conferred with her superiors. She explained the time at which it happened, and then described what she had seen, with the greatest simplicity and accuracy.

Sapientia, who had, so to say, reared her, in whom she had entire confidence, and who, moreover, was, as we have said above, prioress, was

3

naturally the first to whom she had recourse.
Juliana begged of her to declare candidly what
she thought of the vision. Sapientia answered
her that it was a mystery which would be as peril-
ous as it would be uncertain to attempt to discover ; that it was an exceeding rash thing to
endeavour to fathom the secrets of God, that
moreover it was possible that after all it was only
a dream, and that therefore she should dismiss it
from her mind at once, and without further delay.
She then betook herself to persons celebrated for
their piety and sound doctrine, and to whom it
was her duty, or at least a matter of prudence, to
speak of the affair, as for instance her confessor
and the other superiors ; but they replied to her
in the same manner as Sapientia had done.

Juliana endeavoured sincerely to follow the
advice which she knew had been dictated by the
prudence and wisdom of those whom she had consulted. She had too much humility to act otherwise. But although she made a most firm resolution to banish all thoughts of the vision from
her mind, wherever she went, or whatever she did,
it was always present to her, and however strong
her efforts to shut out the vision might be, they
were vain and useless. In order to obtain from
God a cessation of the vision, she spent whole
hours in prayer, fasted and practised every good
work compatible with her state of life, offering up
these good works for the same intention ; but her
prayers were not heard, the vision still continued
to follow her everywhere. She then begged the
prayers of some holy persons with whom she was
acquainted, but neither were their prayers heard.
One of the greatest troubles to her in this matter
was to find that she could not comply with the
wishes of her superiors, who had advised her to
banish the thing altogether from her mind. What

was she to do? She was most anxious to obey, but do what she would, go where she would, the vision was always present. Was it a snare of the demon, craftily laid by him, in order to turn her away from her duties, cast her into trouble, and give her a distaste for her religious exercises? She feared it was, and therefore redoubled her prayers to Almighty God, begging of Him to take away this vision from her. But He heard her not; His time had not yet come. The vision had a meaning; but it was not God's good pleasure to give to her its interpretation at present. Doubtless He wished to exercise her patience, and moreover to show her that it is not for man to fathom His designs, or question His ways, but rather to wait patiently for his God, and in due time God will deliver His helpless creature out of all his troubles.

In the meantime the fame of Juliana's sanctity had spread abroad; for whatever pains she might take to hide her virtue, it was not God's will that it should remain hidden. Now as great virtue is always respected even by worldlings, people began to conceive a high opinion of our saint, and began to respect and revere her as she deserved to be. Sapientia, who had sown in her heart the good seeds of true and solid virtues, which were now bringing forth such marvellous fruits, examined her with the greatest attention, and was obliged to confess that her rapid growth in virtue was to be attributed much more to the extraordinary graces God so abundantly bestowed upon her, than to the care she herself had taken to bring her up in the ways of virtue and sanctity. With her whole heart she praised God for the many favours He bestowed upon her former pupil, and seeing that she corresponded so faithfully with them, she could not refrain from praising her and speaking well of her to all she had occasion to converse with. Juliana was indeed a perfect model of every religious virtue, and Sapientia frequently proposed her to the other sisters as such. They, in their turn, being greatly edified by what they observed in Juliana, were never tired of speaking in her praise, and making her many virtues known to all who came to visit them.

Thus was the fame of Juliana spread abroad, and as it generally happens in such cases, many were desirous to see and speak with her. In spite of her love of solitude and retreat, she could not always refuse to see and speak with those who came to visit her; they who had the good fortune to obtain an interview, always departed with hearts inflamed with the love of God, and full of veneration for His servant; but our humble saint, the more she was esteemed by others, the more did she humble herself in her own eyes, and look upon herself as nothing. To hear herself praised was pain to her, because she knew that all the good she possessed came from God, and that to Him alone was the glory due. When any person with whom she spoke happened to say something to her praise, it only had the effect of making her blush at her own unworthiness, since she was firmly persuaded that she deserved to be treated with contempt, and trodden under foot by all.

The visits of the great were above all a burden to her, so that she avoided them with the greatest care. Whenever it was told her that any rich or noble person requested to see her, she hid herself and kept out of the way as well as she was able. Sometimes it happened that such persons came unexpectedly, so that she could not possibly hide herself, and consequently was obliged to converse with them; then, if they requested her to discourse on divine things, her embarrassment was clearly perceived; notwithstanding this they would ordinarily continue to entreat her to speak to them of God. In such cases the humble spouse of Christ would answer, " I have neither learning nor eloquence to speak to you of the ways of God, I am but a poor, simple nun, having been accustomed all my life to rustic labours ; but since you are both learned and eloquent, be pleased to give me some instruction, and may God reward your charity." Such were the answers she generally made to these requests in her youth; but at a more advanced age, and when she became prioress, not being able to refuse to converse with such people, she answered all their questions with great wisdom and prudence ; she, nevertheless, herself declared that she would rather suffer the pains of purgatory, than the burden of such conversations.

But she did not act in this manner to the poor, who came to her for consolation ; above all, if she had reason to believe that nothing would be said to her in praise of her virtue. To such as these she spoke freely and unrestrainedly ; and as the good man, out of the inward treasure of his heart, bringeth forth good things, so did she, out of a heart overflowing with love for God, bring forth words of such unction, power and efficacy, that the hardest hearts were melted even to tears. She plainly spoke to them of the deformity of vice, and the mournful consequences of its indulgence, since, unless we flee from it, it will in the end inevitably plunge us into the pit of perdition. On the other hand, she would describe to them the beauty of virtue, and the unspeakable peace and joy the practice of it gives even in this life, and the never-ending joys which are its reward in the life to come. If she believed that the rich and the learned knew more than she did, and so, by consequence, preferred to be instructed rather than instruct; her zeal, on the other hand, for those whom she perceived to be rather deficient in religious knowledge, knew no bounds. Her words made so deep an impression on them that they quitted her with difficulty; indeed, such was the force of her burning eloquence, that when she spoke she seemed inspired, and always imparted a balm for every sickness, consolation for every affliction, counsel for every tribulation, and a resource for every necessity. Her every look and movement displayed the glory of grace and a heavenly life.

But while she was receiving honours from without, she was full of troubles within. The vision of which we have spoken was continually present to her view; she had never ceased to beg of God to remove it, but as yet He heard her not. Whether it was a true vision from God, or an illusion of the demon, she knew not; at times when she was persuaded it came from God, she was still troubled, since she could by no means understand its hidden meaning. In this perplexity she resolved to address herself anew to God, and implore Him with all the fervour of which she was capable of showing, to deign either to take away the vision, or reveal to her its mystery. Whenever she had an opportunity of speaking to pious and devout persons, she always begged them to pray for her intention, without however revealing to them what the intention was. Thus, day and night were prayers constantly ascending to the throne of grace for this purpose. Juliana, desiring the removal of every object that could hinder her in the contemplation of the Sovereign Good, was (we may well believe) most fervent in her prayers for this purpose; since she was persuaded that if this state of things should long continue, there would be great danger of its caus-

ing her wearisomeness and disgust in the practice
of her pious exercises. It was for this reason that
she continued so unremittingly to knock at the
gate of the Divine Clemency. As "the prayer
of the just pierceth the clouds," so did Juliana's
prayer at length reach the ear of the Almighty;
He had tried His servant according to His good
pleasure, and was now resolved to grant her petition. One day, therefore, that she was plunged
in deep contemplation, she was on a sudden rapt
in ecstasy, and interiorly heard a voice, like unto
the voice of an angel, speaking to her, and thus
interpreting the vision, telling her that, "the moon
represented the Church, that its lustrous brightness
represented the different solemnities celebrated in
the Church during the course of the year. The
dark spot which obscured a part of the moon's
lustre, signified the want of a certain feast, which
it was God's will should be instituted; that this
feast was to honour the most august and most
holy Sacrament of the Altar; that although the
institution of this venerable sacrament was commemorated on Holy Thursday, yet as upon this
day the Church is so much occupied with the
meditation upon the mystery of our Lord's washing the feet of His disciples, and the commencement of His Passion, as to prevent her from com-
memorating the institution of this adorable sacrament as was meet and proper; it was, therefore,
for these reasons necessary to set apart another
day for this purpose, which should be observed
by all Christendom, and for three reasons. First,
in order that faith in the divine mysteries, which
was growing·cold, and which would grow still
colder in succeeding ages, should be entirely confirmed. Second, in order that men who love and
seek the truth, should have an opportunity of
being instructed therein; and should, moreover,

by the recurrence of this feast, be induced to draw
from this source of life, strength to advance in
the path of perfection. Third, in order that the
irreverences and impieties, which in this Blessed
Sacrament are daily committed against the Divine
Majesty, should be atoned for by a solemn act of
reparation."

Juliana, having had this revelation, was full of
joy and gladness ; but as there is no joy in this
life, which has not also its mixture of sorrow, so
Juliana, in receiving this revelation, was also informed by the same voice which spoke to her interiorly, that she was the instrument chosen by
God, to procure the institution of this Feast in
His Church. This naturally cast the humble
virgin into great trouble, since she could not persuade herself that so great a work was to be
accomplished by so feeble an instrument. She
had solicited the Lord during two years, to be
instructed concerning the truth of the vision ; she
now employed many years in praying to be discharged from the burden of announcing it. This
revelation was vouchsafed to Juliana when she
was only eighteen years of age, which shows with
what rapidity she had run in the way of perfection. But God is always "wonderful in His
saints," raising them up, and favouring them,
because in their own eyes they are poor and lowly,
for God hath respect to the humble and poor, but
beholdeth the proud afar off.

Doubtless, some who profess to pride themselves on possessing strong minds, but whose only
strength generally consists in refusing to believe
what the feebleness of their intellect cannot com-
prehend, will say that this revelation is merely a
dream of one whose brain has been weakened by
practising austerities far beyond the strength of
her tender years. But since the Church has in-

stituted the Feast, if we are not *bound*, we are at
least *permitted* to believe that the vision came
from God. We may do this without fear of being
taxed with over-credulity, since we know how
careful the Church is in such matters : the men
she always employs to investigate things of this
kind, being full of prudence, celebrated for their
learning, as well as for their veracity, probity and
candour. We may feel quite certain that such
men will not easily be deceived, especially when,
(as is nearly always the case,) they expect to meet
with some fraud. Thus, for instance, these theologians do not even regard the foretelling future
events as an evident sign that the vision comes
from God, unless, indeed, it is treated of things
which depend solely on the Divine Will. If the
vision is followed with repose, peace, recollection
of spirit, tender love for God, holy inspirations, a
clear view of the mysteries of faith ; if it inflames
him or her who has the vision with zeal for the
glory of God and the salvation of souls; if it is
accompanied with apparent miracles, that is to
say, with such as do not surpass the power of the
demons; these men tell us that even so we must
not at once conclude that the vision comes from
God. The good dispositions of him or her, who
has had the vision, their well-known piety, their
own testimony to the truth of what they have
seen, the sanctity of the place in which it happened, the novelty of the things they have seen,
all these are *not* signs which exclude every doubt.
These theologians think, and with reason, that in
spite of all these united conditions, illusion is
still possible, because, however holy man may be
here below, he is always subject to error, and because these visions may be caused by the demons,
or by the natural powers, when they have, by

some physical means, been excited in an extraordinary manner.

Before pronouncing any judgment at all, these men, so discreet and so prudent in the discernment of spirits, examine most carefully and thoroughly into the lives of those who have received, or are supposed to have been favoured with visions, according to that admonition of the Holy Spirit: "Believe not every spirit, but try the spirits if they be of God."* They inquire if the persons who are supposed to have revelations, have desired them; if they believe themselves worthy to receive them; if they seek them by curiosity, pride, or to give themselves an appearance of sanctity; if, in the mortifications they practise, they follow their own will; if they publish upon the house top what they suppose God to have revealed to them in secret. In all such cases delusion is to be suspected. But Juliana's case presents none of these signs. She did not desire nor seek after visions, but, on the contrary, begged of God to deliver her from them; nor were her mortifications and penances performed of her own will, for in all things she submitted herself to the will of her superiors. And as for thinking herself worthy to receive such favours, nothing could be further from her thoughts, since she esteemed herself the last and the lowest of all. Again, if they who profess to have received visions are not deeply grounded in humility, and a sense of their own unworthiness and nothingness, if they are only beginners in the spiritual life, if they believe that they have been elevated all at once to the highest degree of contemplation, or hope to attain it by any other means than those of crosses, sufferings, and interior mortification, in all such cases delusion is

* 1 John iv. 1.

to be suspected. But Juliana was most remarkable for her sincere and profound humility; she was not a beginner in the spiritual life, since she had walked in the ways of God from her infancy; moreover, far from shrinking at crosses and sufferings, she desired them ardently, and embraced them joyfully. If visions contain anything contrary to the teachings of Holy Scripture, tradition and the Church, they are to be at once rejected as false. But in this vision of the Blessed Juliana there is nothing of this, because, had there been, the Church would never have instituted the Feast.

But there is one sign by which we may be morally sure that visions come from God, and that is, when assent to them is drawn from those who were not heretofore willing to believe in them, especially when this assent is drawn from them, as it were, against their will. Now this can only happen by the help of God, for it is not in man's power to convince his fellow-man against his will. Now something of this happened in the case of Juliana, for many, (as we shall see,) who at first refused to believe in her vision, did afterwards not only believe in it, but did all they could to procure the establishment of the Feast. Moreover, when visions come from God, they are usually accompanied with an infused light, which, elevating and rendering more subtle that intimate knowledge which every man bears within him, makes known, (to those who are favoured with the vision,) with an entire certainty, the intrinsic truth of the things God has revealed to them, in such a manner that the spirit is perfectly sure of the things it sees, and no longer suspects deception. Now, when God revealed the interpretation of the vision to Juliana, He gave her also this light and knowledge, so that she no longer doubted; but in her inmost heart was perfectly convinced that the

vision came from God ; something like St. Teresa,
when our Lord, in order to dissipate the fears
that her confessor had given her, said to her,
" It is I, fear not," which words fortified her so
much, that every anguish, hesitation and doubt
upon the reality of the vision passed away at the
same moment.   But as this conviction is purely
subjective, the Church, before pronouncing any
judgment, examines thoroughly the effects that
the vision produces in the person who has been so
favoured.   For as this light is supernatural and
divine, its effects ought also to be supernatural
and divine.   Now the Church's decision is only
favourable when she finds in the person who has
received the vision, a full, entire, constant conversion towards good, a perfection such as no creature can attain to by himself, a power for the
performance of good works, such as God alone can
give, a penetrating activity which extends over the
whole life, a constant effort towards a sublime
aim, in relation with the Divine economy relative
to eternal salvation ; when the vision is followed
by marvellous effects, such as miraculous cures
and things of that kind ; when the whole tenor of
the vision, and the aim to which it tends, appears
authentic and divine in its source ; and when he
or she who has received it is perfectly convinced
of its truth.   When the Church finds all these
conditions united, she gives her approbation, and
recommends the vision as worthy of belief.   Now
that the Church has done this much in Juliana's
case, appears from the fact of her having instituted
the Feast ; and no wonder, since her life, and the
conviction she had of the truth of the vision, was,
as we already know, everything that the Church
requires in such cases.   Nor were miracles wanting, as we shall see in the following chapter.
      If we believe that Juliana's vision came from

God, surely we cannot be charged with possessing
weak minds; since we have now seen how strict
and searching an inquiry is always made before
such matters are received as worthy of credit:
that it was so in Juliana's case we shall see further
on.   Nor can we help admiring the supernatural
prudence and wisdom of the Church in these
matters.   The dogmas, doctrines, and principles
of which she is the depositary, have not come to
her by visions, but have been bequeathed to her by
Him who is at once her Spouse, her Founder, her
Head, her Guide; they have been bequeathed to
her by Him who has declared that He will be
with her even unto the consummation of the
world, and who has also assured her that the
"gates of hell itself shall never prevail against
her."   She has received these dogmas, principles,
and doctrines from the mouth of Truth itself;
and He has confided to her the mission of keeping them in all their integrity.   But, on the other
hand, she knows also that the Paraclete has been
promised her, in order to lead her into all truth.
She is aware that the Paraclete acts not only in
the entire body of the Church, but also in each
one of her members in particular; and that thus,
besides the ordinary direction, there is another
which is extraordinary, and which is manifested
in the continuation of the gift of prophecy.   The
Church, therefore, in her wisdom and prudence,
does not neglect the treasures of spiritual wisdom,
knowledge, and contemplation, which, little by
little, in this manner are formed in her bosom
during the course of ages.   Far from neglecting
them, she, on the contrary, esteems them greatly,
and recognizes in them the fruits of that truth
which she already possesses.   But the Church
cannot, for one moment, allow any vision to con-
front her dogmas and teachings, in order thus to

prove the truth of what she teaches; but, on the contrary, she confronts every vision with the truths of which she is the guardian, and without hesitation rejects every vision which is in opposition to her dogmas, or which tends to introduce some new doctrine. Far from supporting herself upon these visions, she it is, on the contrary, who alone has the power to declare that they may be admitted as worthy of credit. It is, therefore, a principle with the Church, to admit these visions and revelations only upon most incontestable proofs. But she is never hasty in deciding; she takes so much time, care, and precaution in examining things of this kind, that the most sceptical, if only he have patience to follow her in her investigations, must be convinced. When some of the proofs which the Church requires in such cases are wanting, she does not at once reject the vision, or revelation, as false, but waits with patience until time, or a more attentive examination, gives her an opportunity of declaring either their truth or falsity. Seeing, then, that the Church, so careful and prudent, has established the feast of Corpus Christi, according as God revealed it to the Blessed Juliana, we surely cannot be either weak-minded or over-credulous in believing that her vision came from God, and was neither the effect of an over-heated imagination, nor a delusion of the demon. That Juliana, to whom our Lord revealed His designs, was a poor, obscure nun;—and, as far as poor, frail, erring human judgment is capable of judging, unfit for so great a work—is nothing to us. God is master of His gifts and graces, and it is not for us poor miserable worms of earth to dare to say to Him: "Why hast Thou done so?" He has done it because He willed it, and because He has the power to do what He wills, to do it when He wills,

and as He wills. Instead, then, of being inclined
to disbelieve, because the one He chose for the
work appears a contemptible instrument, (I mean
appears so in the eyes of worldlings,) let us
rather give thanks to Him because He is "wonderful in His saints," and because "He has hidden these things from the wise and prudent, and
hath revealed them to the little ones."

CHAPTER V.

THE SUPERNATURAL GIFTS BESTOWED UPON ST. JULIANA.

WHAT we have hitherto related of the Blessed
Juliana, may be termed the history of her hidden
life, in which, being unknown to the world, she
was occupied solely with the things of God, and
practising all the virtues of the contemplative life
with the greatest perfection. We have, however,
seen above, that, in spite of her love of silence,
solitude, and retreat, she could not altogether
remain unknown. Now, as those who had already
made her acquaintance were so edified by what
they had observed in her, they everywhere spread
the fame of her sanctity; and thus it was that
she was obliged to hold communication with the
exterior world. But, although compelled to converse with creatures, her heart was always
with God, and so, with whomsoever she conversed,
she sought not to please and flatter them; but
always studied so to speak and act that God
might be glorified, and souls benefited. It is
true she spoke but few words; however, few as

they were, her hearers could not fail to discover the sacred fire which God had enkindled in her soul; when discoursing upon divine things especially, this sacred fire was so manifest and visible, that the hearts of her hearers became all inflamed with love of God. Almighty God bestowed upon her many supernatural graces, by which, in her intercourse with others, she was the better enabled to bring souls to Him. She often penetrated the most secret thoughts of those who came to visit her; frequently foretold future events; healed the sick; and, besides, had a most marvellous faculty of giving consolation to the afflicted; no matter how deep and poignant their grief and anguish might be, if they only had recourse to Juliana they were sure to depart full of consolation.

Among those who in their troubles and doubts came to consult Juliana, was a young virgin whose name was Eva. This holy person, who had hitherto led an irreproachable life, was desirous of becoming a recluse, near the church of St. Martin-on-the-Mount.* But before doing so, as she wished to do nothing rashly, she determined to consult Juliana, (in whom she had great confidence), that she might advise her as to the course she ought to take in this matter. Day by day, Eva felt more and more drawn to the solitary life; but the devil, who dreads nothing so much as the entire dedication of the soul to God, did all in his power to dissuade her from embracing this kind of life. He drew a most flattering picture of the world and its pleasures on the one hand; and

* The Collegiate Church of St. Martin-au-Mont, at Liège, was founded in 963, by Eraclius, Bishop of Liège. The bishop was dangerously ill, and his life being despaired of, he, in this extremity, invoked the aid of St. Martin. The saint appeared to him in his sleep, touched him with his staff, and the bishop was immediately restored to health. Out of gratitude for so signal a favour, he founded a church in honour of St. Martin.

on the other, filled her mind with the most exaggerated pictures of the horrors of solitude; then, if she banished these thoughts, he endeavoured to persuade her that as she was naturally frail and delicate, she would never be able to endure the austerity of the life she proposed to embrace, and so would, in the end, be obliged to return to the world. He would then paint in the most vivid colours, the great humiliation she would experience in being compelled to return to the world, after having made a fruitless attempt to lead a solitary life. Eva did not know whether prudence suggested these thoughts, or if it was the enemy of all salvation, who was thus by artful ruses endeavouring to turn her from her holy purpose. It was when she was in this trouble and perplexity that she had recourse to our saint. Juliana, after a careful examination of her dispositions, was fully persuaded that Eva's call to the solitary life was really from God. She therefore used all her eloquence to persuade Eva to break at once with the world and all its deceitful charms; nor were her words without effect, for scarcely had the saint began to speak to her, than she was resolved to accomplish her pious design, cost what it might; all the dark clouds which had hitherto darkened her mind, vanished, and light, peace, and serenity returned. Before parting, however, they made a mutual promise to pray for each other, to act towards each other without the least reserve, telling even their most secret thoughts, which was for Eva a great consolation. Besides this, Juliana was to visit her friend at least once a year. Thus was laid the foundation of a friendship which lasted until death.

The life led by these recluses was, in general, very austere, and entirely contemplative. They

4

could speak only to their confessor, or ecclesiastics
of well-known piety and probity; and this not
without the permission of those who directed
them. Their time was spent in prayer and other
pious exercises, and in manual labour; but they
so laboured with their hands, that their minds
and hearts were at the same time elevated to God.
Eva appears to have been under the direction of
the Cistercian Fathers, since we find that mention
is made of her in the Cistercian Menologium,
on June 25th, in these words: "At Liège died
the Blessed Eva, recluse of the *Cistercian Order*,
who, together with the Blessed Juliana, promoted
with wonderful fervour the institution of the
solemnity of the Blessed Sacrament, and who,
rendered illustrious by many celestial revelations
and favours, hath passed away to the kingdom of
heaven."*

But this is only one instance out of many, in
which Juliana was the means of bringing peace to
the troubled mind. For none were more proper
to counsel the doubtful and console the afflicted
than Juliana. A religious, who had lost a relative
whom she exceedingly loved, abandoned herself to
so much sorrow on this account, that nothing was
capable of assuaging her grief; everything was
painful to her, every exercise seemed to cause her
loathing and disgust; her grief, instead of dimin-
ishing, seemed every day to increase, and at length
reached to such a degree, that she fell into a state
bordering on frenzy. Many remedies were employed to alleviate her anguish, but all in vain.
At length she addressed herself to Juliana, discovered to her the state of her soul, and begged of
her to intercede with God on her behalf. Juliana
was, no doubt, deeply grieved to find such a want

---

* Men. Cist. p. 207.

of resignation to the Will of God in one of those dedicated in a special manner to His love and service. But she was too discreet and prudent to manifest any surprise at the strange conduct of this religious; whatever Juliana might have thought of such conduct, it is certain she pitied this poor soul, and prayed most fervently for her to God. She therefore began by sympathizing with her in her affliction; then she spoke to her of resignation to the Will of God, which is always holy, wise, just and good; then represented to her the instability of all human things; that God alone should be the foundation of all our happiness; that we must be attached to Him alone; and that He is the only sure and certain remedy for all our woes. Then she described to her the great advantage we derive from submitting ourselves to the Divine Providence in all the events of our mortal life; that by doing so we find an inexhaustible source of consolation, comfort and sweetness, since out of Him all is trouble, darkness and distress. This discourse of the Blessed Juliana took immediate effect; the religious perceived that all her pain, anguish and grief had vanished, not little by little, but suddenly and entirely. To her former trouble and vexation succeeded so sensible a joy, that she was herself in utter astonishment at such a wonderful change; and she everywhere declared that it was impossible to behold a more marvellous transformation than that which she had so suddenly experienced. It was doubtless the work of the Most High, Who had listened to the prayers which His servant Juliana had offered for this poor soul, and Who was thus pleased to manifest the sanctity of His servant.

In Juliana was accomplished those words of our Lord: "I have called you friends, because all things whatsoever I have heard of My Father, I have made known to you." Almighty God bestowed upon her the gift of prophecy, and the knowledge of the hearts of men, which knowledge He ordinarily reserves to Himself alone. We who walk in the lower paths of the spiritual life can only see with our corporal eyes, and consequently, can only see material things; everything spiritual and supernatural is hidden from our view. But with the saints it is far otherwise; the interior eye of their soul is opened to spiritual things. When, after having closed our eyes, we turn them to the sun, we can still feel its heat, and have only to open them in order to behold its rays. So it is with the saints; the eye of their souls is always turned to the Sun of Justice, and as they never close this interior eye, but keep it constantly fixed on this Divine Sun, no wonder it sees things that to the exterior eye are a mystery. We usually open our exterior and corporal eyes, to gaze upon all that can give us a momentary and fleeting pleasure, but trouble ourselves little to open the interior eye of the soul, and fix it upon God and things of eternity. The saints do the very contrary; they mortify the corporal sense of sight in every way, and God oftentimes rewards them by elevating their spiritual sight in a marvellous degree. They are so dead to all material things, that they see and hear God alone; being deaf to every noise that the world endeavours to make them hear, no inspiration of God escapes them. God, on His part, seems to take delight in communicating to them His secrets; He gives Himself to them, according to the measure they have given themselves to Him. God is in them, no longer simply by that general presence, by which His Essence is in all, but by that particular presence, wherewith He enlightens the spirit with His light, and draws it with His love. "If any man love Me," saith our Lord, "and keepeth My commandments, My Father also will love him, and We will come to him, and will make our abode with him." This is what happens in that mysterious union of the saints with God. They are, in this state, only one spirit with God, not in a substantial manner, it is true, (for then they would be united to Him hypostatically,) but by an intimate transformation. Being thus transformed in God, they become accustomed to look at all things in Him, and He shewing them whatever He deems expedient for their own and others' salvation, they become acquainted with things that cannot be known by natural means, but which they behold in a supernatural manner, by consequence of their close and intimate union with God. It was doubtless in this manner that the Blessed Juliana was enabled to read the hearts of others, see things that were passing at a distance, and foretell future events; a few examples of which we are now going to give, though when we consider that six hundred years have passed away since she was consigned to the tomb, we may feel quite certain that very many interesting facts of this kind are lost to us, but enough still remains to shew us that she was, like other saints, favoured with many graces of this kind.

A recluse, whose name was Hauvide, lived at Liège, in great sanctity, in the parish of St. Remacle-au-Pont, near to Mount Cornillon. This holy recluse had frequent conversations with Juliana, and she assures us that Juliana had foretold her many things which afterwards came to pass. Among other things she said that Hauvide would survive both her mother and sister, which happened as she had predicted.

Juliana went one day, out of charity, to visit a

priest who was known to her, and who was dangerously ill. She, however, only remained a moment with him ; she assured him that her only reason for departing so soon was, that she knew very well he would soon be restored to health; then, recommending him to communicate every eight days during his convalescence, she returned to her convent. Her prediction was fulfilled to the letter, the priest was speedily restored. Although the sick man was in delirium when Juliana visited him, yet he perfectly understood all she had said, and failed not to follow her counsel relative to communicating every eight days during his convalescence.

Eva, the recluse, in the commencement of her solitary life, suffered greatly from the violent assaults of the devil. He tempted her in every way, allowing her no peace day or night. At first, Eva combated the temptations of the evil one with great patience and fortitude ; but at length his assaults became so violent and horrible, that she began to fear that in the end he would prevail. In this distress of mind Eva had recourse to her good friend Juliana ; now the latter, knowing very well that God permitted His servant to be tempted in this manner, in order that she might be purified in the furnace of tribulation, and knowing, moreover, that God had chosen her to be one of His most faithful spouses, she exhorted Eva to bear this trial with patience, and not to allow herself to be cast down or overcome by any snares of the wicked one, however artfully and skilfully he might set them. She also foretold her that this trial would be of short duration, which happened as she had prophesied. For the storm, which had hitherto been so violent as to threaten shipwreck, abated, the winds and the rain ceased, and there was a great calm. Eva attributed the profound tranquillity she now experienced, to the prayers of her friend Juliana.

Upon one occasion, some important affairs belonging to the house having to be transacted at a considerable distance, they sent a priest for this purpose to the place. It was winter, the cold exceedingly intense, and the ground so covered with snow, that there did not remain the least trace of the roads. On this account the priest lost his way, and came so suddenly upon the border of a precipice, that he must have infallibly perished, had he not been miraculously preserved. But God had revealed the imminent peril of this good priest to Juliana, and she quickly caused the sisters to be assembled, in order that they might pray for his deliverance, which they did with all possible fervour. Juliana again learning by revelation that the danger had passed, they returned thanks to God for His great mercy in delivering the priest from the great peril which had threatened him. When he returned to Cornillon, he related the great dangers he had run, and the sudden and miraculous manner in which he had been delivered. Upon comparing the hour and the moment in which he had been delivered, they found it the very same in which Juliana had caused the sisters to be assembled to pray for him, and all praised God Who had bestowed such wonderful graces upon His servant.

On one occasion that Eva the recluse was sick, Juliana hearing of it, went to visit her; but before entering Eva's cell she went into the church to pray, then immediately she saw the recluse, she told her that she would soon recover from her sickness, which came to pass as she had foretold. Doubtless this had been revealed to her in the church by God, in order that she might impart consolation to her friend. They then began to

discourse together, and Eva was surprised at the
things our saint foretold, the accomplishment of
which was witnessed some years after by the
recluse herself.

A sister of the community, whose name was
Ozila, had a severe affection of the throat, which
prevented her from taking any solid nourishment;
the sickness was so grievous that she could not
even receive the Holy Communion. Now, as she
had an earnest desire to communicate, they resolved that if she was not able to do so, she
should, at least, have the happiness of adoring
her Lord; for this purpose the Blessed Sacrament
was carried to the cell of the sick sister. Juliana,
(who was occupied with some labour outside the
house, in company with some other sisters,) hearing the signal which is usually given when Communion is carried to the sick, prostrated upon the
ground, and prayed the Lord to give Sister Ozila
the grace to communicate. Then, rising up, she
begged her companions to return thanks to Almighty God, because He had so far alleviated the
sickness of their sister as to enable her to communicate. Upon their return to the house, they
found that the thing had happened precisely as
Juliana had said.

She had also the faculty of perceiving the presence of the Holy Eucharist, even at a great distance. When Eva, her friend, visited her, Juliana
often remarked that they took away the Blessed
Sacrament from the church of St. Martin after
the divine service, and each time she experienced
great sadness from it. Eva, upon her return,
would always find that this had really been the
case.

Juliana was always willing to console those in
trouble and affliction, even when, as was sometimes the case, she herself had to suffer inconve-

nience in doing so. Upon one occasion, that she was in bed oppressed with great languor, which had been brought on by the vehemence of her love for God, a poor young woman was desirous to speak with her; she was told that Juliana was sick, and unable to come to her, but the poor girl pleaded so hard with the sisters to tell Juliana she wished to see her, that at length they consented. Juliana, (who doubtless knew that this soul stood in need of comfort,) though, at the time, too weak to rise from her bed, begged the sisters to send the poor girl to her. They did so; as soon as she saw her, she said to her: "Approach, let us speak of God, but before doing so, let us invoke the help and assistance of the Holy Trinity, three times, in order that our conversation may bring joy to our hearts, and elevate them to our Celestial Spouse." This invocation was scarcely concluded, than the young girl suddenly experienced such an extraordinary suavity that she could not moderate its abundance. Her soul seemed to be immersed in an ocean of delights; she was, as it were, in ecstasy, out of herself, surrounded with beatitude; so powerfully did grace act upon her in that moment.

The charity of Juliana was not limited to the relief and comfort of the living, it was also extended to the poor suffering souls in purgatory. She knew that these souls were dearly loved by God, and that they were destined one day to enjoy His blissful presence. She knew how ardently they longed and sighed for the day of their deliverance; that they were utterly unable to help themselves, and that they could only be assisted and solaced by the suffrages of the living. It seemed to her that she constantly heard these poor suffering souls crying out in the words of holy Job: "Have pity upon me, have pity upon

me, at least you my friends, for the hand of the
Lord hath touched me." It was for these reasons
that the Blessed Juliana employed all sorts of
means for the relief of these suffering spouses of
her Lord ; prayer, fasting, and other macerations
of the body. She was frequently apprised of the
success of her prayers, by extraordinary ways.
One day, that she was conversing with the same
poor girl of whom we spoke in the preceding
paragraph, she stopped suddenly in her discourse,
and said, "My dear sister, let us pray for the
soul of one of my friends, who has just this moment expired." Upon the other inquiring how
she could possibly know this, Juliana answered :
"At the moment in which a person of my acquaintance has expired, I am seized with pains so
violent, that it seems almost impossible for me to
bear them. I have often found, upon comparing
the hour of their decease with that in which I
was attacked with these violent pains, that it was
exactly the same." She frequently learnt, by
Divine revelation, the passage of a soul from this
world into eternity, especially if the soul stood in
need of prayers. One day, a lady who had lost her
sister, having come to Cornillon to visit Juliana,
the latter, as soon as she saw the lady, said to
her, "You have lost your sister, and I have prayed
for her." At these words the lady was greatly
astonished, since she knew full well that Juliana
could not possibly have learned this by any human
means.

But of all the miraculous graces Almighty God
bestowed upon the Blessed Juliana, there was
none 'by which she could benefit the soul of her
neighbours more, than by the faculty she had of
penetrating the hearts of others. For this enabled her to apply proper remedies to the diseases
of the souls of those with whom she conversed.

Thus, when speaking with those whom by this means she recognised to be of a proud and haughty disposition, she spoke so movingly, and with so much grace and unction, on the virtue of Christian humility, that by this means many, being conscience-stricken, renounced for ever their pride, and walked henceforth in the path of holy humility. When by this supernatural instinct she recognised in any of those who visited her the vices of envy, sloth, lust, or avarice, she always spoke of their opposite virtues with so much tact, prudence, and eloquence, that her hearers, without being offended at what she said, nevertheless, could not but be fully aware of the reason of her speaking in so touching a manner upon these virtues, and many were by this means converted to God. She, however, if compelled to speak of the defects of her neighbour, did all she could to hide the grace God had bestowed upon her in thus being able to read their most secret thoughts; and she spoke with so much circumspection, that they never failed to be edified with her discourse, and nearly always quitted her with regret. We say nearly always, for of course there were occasions upon which she was misunderstood; the devil always seeking to frustrate the work of God as much as possible. A great lord, who had heard many things said of the extraordinary sanctity of Juliana, (and who consequently looked upon her as the personification of every virtue,) determined to visit her. He did so, and during his conversation with her, he spoke at length of the crimes which were committed in the world. Juliana wept over them bitterly, and remarked that in every state of life human nature was weak and feeble. He, thinking that she intended the remark for himself, was highly indignant, and went away greatly offended; thus giving, in his own person, a proof of the truth of Juliana's assertion, since he was himself so weak that he could not hear the simple truth without taking offence and losing his temper.

Juliana having one day gone to visit her friend Eva, the recluse of St. Martin's, she begged her to tell her without disguise all that she had in her heart. Eva, forgetting for the moment the agreement they had made together, was surprised at such an interrogation, and stood astonished and amazed, not knowing what to answer. Juliana said to her, "What is the matter, sister? Do you think I am ignorant of that which is passing through your mind? Believe me, I know your thoughts as well as if I had them written in the palm of my hand." She then wrote a few characters upon the ground, to make known to her that she could hide nothing from her. Then, to Eva's great astonishment, she discovered to her the most secret and hidden thoughts and intentions of her heart.

Some impostors having returned from the Holy Land, related to different pious persons, and among others to a gentleman at Liège, that they knew where the pillar was to which our Lord was bound during His flagellation; also, that they knew where the whips and other precious relics were. But when Juliana was consulted as to her opinion upon the matter, she declared that it was an imposition. Her words were verified, for the persons who were charged to make an examination upon the affair, proved the falsehood of the impostures, for which they were severely punished.

Many persons had recourse to Juliana, not only in their spiritual, but also in their corporal pains; the fame of her sanctity had so spread abroad, that many were fully persuaded that if they desired to be delivered from their miseries they had only to apply to Juliana. Nor were they deceived in their expectations, for many were by her restored to health, and what was of still greater benefit to those who received the favour, many whom it was God's good pleasure to leave in the furnace of affliction, through Juliana's prayers, obtained the grace to pass through the trial with a patience and resignation truly heroic, thus laying up for themselves an abundance of treasures in heaven, which would infinitely outweigh all the sufferings of this mortal life. Juliana's great charity rendered her sensible to the corporal, as well as spiritual, infirmities of her neighbours, and putting herself in the place of the afflicted persons, she would represent to herself how she would wish to be solaced in her pains, if she was suffering as they were. If God, therefore, did not at first hear her prayers on their behalf, her charity was so great, that she would importune Him, by prayers, fastings, and macerations of the body, until she had obtained either their perfect cure, or such an abundance of grace that their afflictions became rather a source of joy, than pain and sorrow.

A religious, who had served God many years in the convent, having unfortunately relaxed from her first fervour, her conduct was anything but edifying. She was full of weariness and disgust for her religious exercises ; nothing was heard from her lips but murmurs and impatient exclamations. The spiritual exercises of the community were a burden ; conversation with her sisters made her only more fretful, and more discontented ; wherever she went she was sure to see something that displeased her ; whatever she had to do was pain and grief to her ; she was disgusted with everything and everybody. But God, Who is rich in mercy, had pity on this poor soul, and as He frequently makes use of His own creatures to bring souls to Himself, so upon this occasion He made use of Juliana to convert this soul from a state of tepidity to fervour. He, therefore, put it into the mind of this poor religious to have recourse to Juliana ; for once she listened to an inspiration of grace, and did so. She exposed to Juliana her state of tepidity, and our Saint, being at once interested in her case, prayed as if it had been herself who was in this dangerous state, and thus obtained from God the fervour which was so much needed by this religious. She afterwards invited her to come and speak with her ; then taught her, with that sweetness and charity for which she was so remarkable, the way in which to perform her duties, so as to be pleasing to God, and, at the same time, accomplished with joy and gladness. But the religious complained that she was constantly suffering from violent pains in the head, by which she was often utterly incapable of giving herself to prayer and meditation. Juliana then placed her veil upon the head of the nun, and her pains ceased at once, and for ever.

A religious had a tumour upon her eyes which caused her excessive pain, and which had also very much deformed her. During two years she had been under medical treatment without obtaining the least relief, so that no hope of any cure seemed to remain. She therefore determined to have recourse to Juliana. The Saint, after saying a few words to her on some ordinary subject, made the sign of the cross over her eyes, and then presented to the religious a handkerchief with which she was accustomed to wipe away her tears which she shed in the fervour of her prayers. The next day, when assisting at the Holy Sacrifice of the Mass, the religious slept, and it seemed to her that a venerable old man had taken away the tumour. Upon awaking, she found that the pain, which before was intense and almost unbearable, had entirely ceased; she then put her hand to her face, and found that every vestige of the deformity had entirely disappeared. She at once gave thanks to God, Who, by the hands of His servant Juliana, had wrought this wonder.

But in the midst of this intercourse with creatures, she never, for one moment, forgot her Creator; her heart was constantly united to Him, and even during the most distracting occupations she always kept Him in view. If this was so during her state of action, (and it was,) what may we not imagine was her fervour when engaged in the holy exercises of prayer and contemplation? It was at these times especially, that being no longer embarrassed and constrained by the presence of creatures, she became oblivious of earth and earthly things, and was plunged in the deepest contemplation of the One Sole Object of all her desires. One day, that she was reciting the Canonical Hours with another sister, as they came to the doxology, she all at once fixed her eyes on heaven, and was ravished in the contemplation of the adorable mystery of the Blessed Trinity. It seemed to her that she saw most clearly the glory of the heavenly Jerusalem; and contemplating the different Orders of the Celestial Spirits, Virgins, Confessors, Martyrs, Apostles, Prophets, Patriarchs, Angels and Archangels, Cherubim, Seraphim, and all the Hosts of Heaven, she was elevated even to the contemplation of the beauty and perfections of the Most Holy Trinity. She was rapt in admiration of the celestial beatitude the saints enjoy in the bosom of God, and the ocean of eternal delights in which they are immersed; then casting a look upon earth, she con-

gratulated herself in possessing the Sovereign
Good in the most august Sacrament of the Altar.
She, in that moment, contemplated the marvellous
graces and the amazing depths of God's love for
man, which are displayed in this thrice-blessed
Sacrament of His love ; God's love for man as
manifested in this Sacrament being so great, that
it is impossible for him either to conceive the
extent of this love, or render to God the devotion,
gratitude and love which are due to Him for so
great a gift. She was frequently favoured by God
with these ecstasies ; but as her faith in the mysteries of our holy religion was a firm and lively
faith, and as her heart was wounded with Divine
love, we need not be surprised that, in the heat
and fervour of her contemplations, she was totally
forgetful of all earthly things, and wholly rapt in
the love and admiration of God, and the mysteries
of His love. Indeed, her faith was so firm and
lively, that it seemed to her a most astonishing
thing, that there should be any heresies in the
world ; she could not understand how it was that
anyone could refuse to submit themselves to that
authority which Christ Himself has established on
earth, since, in doing so, it is impossible to fall
into error, for He Himself has promised to be
with His Church until the end of time, and if
Truth itself is with her, how can she fall into
error ? Thus, amidst all the favours God bestowed upon Juliana, or rather, we may doubtless
say, because of them, she always remained a sub-
missive and humble daughter of the Church.

One of her greatest consolations was to converse with Eva, the recluse of St. Martin's, whom
she looked upon as her spiritual daughter, and
whom she had begotten in Christ. Upon one
occasion, our Saint went to visit her friend on the
Vigil of the Feast of the Dedication of the Church

of St. Martin. She was not, however, aware of this, until told of it by her friend; no sooner did she hear it than she sprang towards the window of the cell, which looked into the church, with so much zeal and emotion, that she would inevitably have been precipitated into the church, had not her friend Eva retained her. Juliana then perceiving upon the wall an image of Jesus Crucified, was suddenly seized with such violent sorrow, that she fell upon the ground as dead, nor did there remain the least sign of life in her. Eva raised her up, and placed her upon the bed; when she had a little returned to herself, Eva endeavoured to console her by reminding her that Jesus Christ, now in possession of His glory, no longer suffered. "Yes," answered Juliana, "I know this, but has He not suffered for us torments and sufferings so great, so immense, as to demand in return all our love and all our gratitude?" The Feast having been announced by the ringing of the great bell of the church, Juliana fixed her eyes upon heaven, and was so absorbed in contemplation, that any one observing her would have thought her soul had already departed from the body. Eva at this moment looked at her attentively, and perceived that her body was so motionless, that there did not appear the least sign of life. The only signs of life that could be observed were, the supernatural brilliancy of her eyes, and the heavenly expression of her countenance. Her complexion was white and fair as a lily; her cheeks, which before were pale, were now tinted with a beautiful vermilion; her eyes were more brilliant and shining than the most sparkling gems, and were clear as crystal. It seemed to Eva that she was speaking with the holy Apostles SS. Peter and Paul; she was still more convinced of this, when Juliana, returning from her rapture,

5

cried out : " Let us go, let us go."   " And where
do you wish to go ?" said Eva to her. " To
Rome," she replied, " to visit the tomb of the
Apostles."

The keenest pain that Juliana experienced was
caused by the offences that are daily committed
against the Divine Majesty ; she never ceased to
weep over the sins of men in general, and her own
in particular ; for she always esteemed herself the
greatest sinner in the world, and frequently requested her friends, and above all, Eva, to beg of
God to be merciful to her. If Juliana, who was
so exceedingly innocent, pure and holy, thus
esteemed herself, what ought we to think of ourselves; we are so weak and frail that we oftentimes
succumb to the most trifling temptation.   We
know that the saints did not speak in this manner
of themselves through any sentiment of exaggera-
tion, but simply because they believed what they
said ; and because, having great lights, they saw
the deformity of sin much clearer than we do.
Thus, if we enter a room when the sun is not
shining through the windows, we do not perceive
any particles of dust in the air ; but if the sun
suddenly shines through the windows, then, wherever its rays pierce, we see by their assistance
thousands of small particles of dust floating about.
So it is with the saints ; their minds being illu-
mined with the Sun of Justice, by the help of His
Divine rays, which pierce through their inmost
souls, they perceive things which altogether escape
our notice.   Moreover, by reason of their corres-
pondence with the grace of God, they receive these
rays of light much more frequently, and in greater
abundance than we do.

But if Juliana received from God so many
lights and graces, she had sufferings too in proportion.   In addition to bodily pains, and an

excessive weakness and languor from which she almost constantly suffered, she had also to endure mental pains. The devil, enraged beyond measure at seeing himself deprived of so many souls, who, through the prayers and exhortations of this humble virgin, were snatched out of his hand, determined to leave her neither rest nor peace. Our Blessed Lord, who permitted Himself to be tempted by this spirit of darkness, permitted also this malignant spirit to persecute His servant. The infernal fiend, therefore, laid for Juliana all the snares that his malice could suggest; he scarcely ever left her one moment in peace; now assaulting her in one way, now in another. No sooner had she overcome one trial, than, still more enraged than before, he would lay his snares with all the cunning, craft, and subtlety he could command; ever seeking to draw her into that abyss of woe and misery into which his pride has precipitated himself. But Juliana, who had taught so many others to resist all the "fiery darts of the wicked one," was not herself to be vanquished by him. In this her trouble she had recourse to Him Who is the secure and ever-ready help in time of trouble; to Him did she cry, and He delivered her out of all her distress; in Him she placed all her hope and trust, and was not confounded. It was, above all, in the Sacrament of the Altar that she sought for strength to fight against her enemy; at this time, therefore, she received more frequently than usual the Holy Communion, and, fortified with the Bread of Life, she triumphed gloriously over the enemy of her salvation. Thus did she experience that the just who put their trust in God will most assuredly be protected by Him; and that, "he that dwelleth in the aid of the Most High, shall abide under the protection of the God of Heaven. He shall say to the Lord : Thou art my protector and my refuge : my God, in Him will I trust. For He hath delivered me from the snare of the hunters, and from the sharp word. He will overshadow thee with His shoulders ; and under His wings shalt thou trust. His truth shall compass thee with a shield : thou shalt not be afraid of the terror of the night, of the arrow that flieth by day : ....of invasion, or of the noon-day devil......... Because Thou, O Lord, art my hope : thou hast made the Most High thy refuge. There shall no evil come to thee ; nor shall the scourge come near thy dwelling. For He hath given His angels charge over thee, to keep thee in all thy ways. In their hands they shall bear thee up, lest thou dash thy foot against a stone. Thou shalt walk upon the asp and the basilisk : and thou shalt trample underfoot the lion and the dragon. Because he hoped in Me I will deliver him : I will protect him because he hath known My name. He shall cry to Me, and I will hear him : I am with him in tribulation. I will deliver him, and I will glorify him. I will fill him with length of days ; and I will show him My salvation."*

* Psalm xc.

CHAPTER VI.

ST. JULIANA IS ELECTED PRIORESS.

HITHERTO we have had occasion simply to speak of Juliana as a subject, and we have seen with what zeal, fervour, and perfection she performed her duties as such; how she was to all a model of regularity, piety, simplicity, obedience, and of every virtue. But we have now to speak of her as a superioress, and we shall see that in this capacity also, she accomplished all her duties with such zeal and charity, such fervour and prudence, such wisdom and discretion, that St. Benedict himself would have recognised her as a superioress full of the spirit of his rule.

Sapientia, the prioress of Cornillon, died the death of the just in the year 1222, to the great regret of all her children, who loved and revered her, as she justly deserved to be. She is mentioned in the Cistercian Menologium; and all who have written the life of Juliana, have spoken of this holy woman in terms of the highest commendation. The name of Sapientia was fitly bestowed upon her, for she was truly wise, (Sapientia means wisdom), not indeed with the wisdom of the world, but with the true wisdom of the children of God. She had ruled the souls committed to her care well and wisely, (some, however, as we shall presently see, had not profited by her wholesome admonitions,) she had been a good mother to all; she had, as an old author remarks, " fed their bodies as a nurse, and refreshed their souls as a mistress of the spiritual life, by teaching them, and instructing them in the law of life and love." She had taught her children to " draw waters with joy out of the Saviour's fountains;" and if she was grieved to find that some did not follow her wise teachings, she had the consolation of seeing others profit by them, and attain a high degree of sanctity. She had embraced the Cistercian institute in her youth, and had persevered in the observance of its holy laws until death ; she was, indeed, a woman adorned with great virtues, wisdom, and discretion; and God took her out of this troublesome and wicked world, to bestow upon her, in reward for her great virtue and holiness, a crown of glory which shall never fade away. We may well believe that Juliana keenly felt the loss of one who had been to her more than a mother; but however deeply she may have felt it, she was too resigned to the holy Will of God to allow it to interfere, even in the least degree, with that close and intimate union with God which had now become her habitual state.

Sapientia being now no more, and the house without a prioress, it became the duty of the sisters to elect one to fill her place. The virtues of Juliana being so well known to all, it seemed to them that no one was more fitting to occupy the place of their beloved deceased mother than our saint. She was, therefore, by the unanimous voice of the sisters, elected prioress. Doubtless, the humble virgin would infinitely have preferred to have been sent back to her old employment of keeping the cows, but the sisters would take no denial, they had elected her to be their mother and their mistress; and however much Juliana may have loved to obey, and submit herself to others, she was now compelled to undertake the office of ruling and governing those committed to her care.

The fact of Juliana having been chosen for such an office, at so early an age, gives us an evident proof of the eminence of her virtue and sanctity; since, if these virtues and sanctity had not been very great and well known to the sisters, they would never have passed over those whose age and wisdom fully qualified them for the duties of Superioress, and chosen one who was scarcely thirty years of age.

Juliana entered upon her new duties with a due sense of the awful responsibility of such an office; she ever remembered that she should one day have to give a strict account of "her entire administration," and "that she would most certainly have to answer on the day of judgment for every individual soul committed to her care, and for her own soul in addition." These words of St. Benedict were constantly ringing in her ears, and exciting her to greater fervour in the performance of her duties. She had naturally a great love of souls, and an ardent desire to bring them to Christ; but now that she was bound by her office to excite her children to the practice of virtue, her zeal knew no bounds. She entirely cast aside all the privileges that her office might have procured her; she was far more the servant of all, than the mistress. St. Benedict, in the second chapter of his Holy Rule, in which he speaks of the duties and responsibilities of the Abbot or Superior, says: "He who is appointed to the Abbatial office should instruct his subjects by a two-fold manner of preaching; that is, he should teach them all that is good and holy, more by his deeds than by his words. To such as are well disposed, or of good understanding, he should announce the law of God verbally; but to those of weak capacity, and to the hard-hearted, he should preach it by his works." Now this advice

of our holy father, Juliana followed to the letter;
for the patient and the meek, a word, nay, a look
was sufficient, so great was their love for her ; but
if she noticed any whose docility and submission
were not yet quite perfect, she never imposed upon
them any duty without first showing them in her
own person, an example of the manner in which
it should be performed. Such as these she sought
to draw to God by using all the gentleness and
sweetness of her angelic disposition ; in all her
commands to them she never allowed the least
spirit of domination or authority to appear ; so
that they were forced to admire in her the humility of a servant, the tender care of a nurse, and
the charity of a superioress, who was an enemy of
everything which is calculated to make the yoke
of inferiority heavy and burdensome. She caused
her subjects to obey her rather through love than
fear.

The sisters had so great confidence in the wisdom and prudence of Juliana, that it was to her
they had recourse in all their pains, doubts, difficulties, trials and temptations ; nor was their confidence misplaced, for, in addressing themselves
to her, they were sure to receive consolation ; and
the succour that they always obtained through her
prayers was as prompt, as it was efficacious. She
consoled the afflicted, animated the feeble, instructed, encouraged and assisted the pusillani-
mous, stimulated the fervent to still greater fervour, and excited others to imitate them. She
endeavoured to inspire all her children with an
ardent desire of perfection, a love of solitude, recollection and prayer, and above all, a great devotion to the Most Holy Sacrament of the Altar.
She exhorted them without ceasing to endeavour
to acquire as close and intimate a union with God
as is possible for man here below to attain, and

thus to begin here on earth that contemplation and love of God, which is to be our everlasting occupation in heaven.

Love and union being most essential to the religious life, the holy prioress frequently spoke to her daughters of the excellence and beauty of that charity which "never falleth away," and which "beareth all things, believeth all things, hopeth all things, endureth all things." She was mindful of those beautiful words of the Royal Psalmist: "Behold how good and joyful a thing it is for brethren to dwell together in unity. It is like the precious ointment on the head, that ran down upon the beard, the beard of Aaron, and went down to the skirts of his clothing. It is like the dew of Hermon, which fell upon the hill of Sion. For there the Lord hath commanded blessing and life for evermore."* As, then, charity and union are so essential to the well-being of a religious community, and so pleasing to God, Juliana did all that lay in her power to bind her children together, in the bonds of love and peace; and if she noticed in any of them any little discord, or if any complaint was made to her of such, she immediately applied herself to re-establish peace and concord, and was full of joy whenever she saw it reign in the entire house. In her public and private discourses, she ever exhorted her daughters to gratitude to God, for the great grace He had conferred upon them, in bringing them to the secure harbour of holy religion, and reminded them that in return for so great a gift, they should endeavour to be like the angels in purity, and like the seraphim, all burning with love for Jesus Christ their Spouse; and, moreover, that as vir-

* Psalm cxxxii.

gins consecrated to the Lord, they were bound to
be an example to others of every virtue.

The sick and infirm were the special objects of
her care and solicitude; she was not unmindful of
the great care and attention that St. Benedict
requires to be shown to them. He thus speaks of
the sick in the thirty-sixth chapter of his holy
Rule: "Before and above all, let care be taken of
the sick; let them be served as Christ Himself;
for He hath said, 'I was sick, and you visited
Me.' And again, 'As long as you did it to one
of these My least brethren, you did it to Me.'*
.........The Abbot will, therefore, take all possible
care that they be in no wise neglected..........The
Abbot will adopt every precaution, lest the sick
should be neglected by the Procurator, or those
appointed to serve them, for he shall be held
responsible for their negligence." Accordingly,
Juliana had great charity for these suffering members of Jesus Christ, doing all she could to soothe
their pain, and alleviate their anguish. Nor was
it merely in a corporal manner that she came to
their assistance, but she taught them also how to
bear their afflictions with resignation and patience,
telling them to unite their little sufferings with
the immense ocean of pain and anguish our dear
Lord hath endured for love of us, and, moreover,
reminding them, "that our tribulation (in this
life) worketh for us above measure exceedingly, an
eternal weight of glory."†

We might naturally suppose that so much
charity on the part of a superioress so holy would
have gained every heart; but it was not so: God
so permitting it, in order that the patience of His
servant might be tried, and her great virtue be
manifested to all. We have said above, that there

---

* Matt. xxv. 36, 40.   † 1 Cor. iv. 17.

were some sisters whom Sapientia could never, with all her pious exhortations, bring to a true sense of their duty; but who, to the day of her death, had been a thorn in her side, and a source of pain, grief and sorrow. But Juliana, before she had been elected prioress, had been so intent on, and rapt in the contemplation of God, and in attention to the things belonging to her soul's salvation, that she had never noticed anything of this. The majority of the sisters were, indeed, models of every religious perfection; but these few relaxed ones, who were of a harsh, sharp, cross disposition, severely tried the patience of our Saint. Since Juliana had been elected unanimously, we must suppose that either, for once in their lives, they had acted conscientiously, or that they had given their voices in favour of Juliana, because they thought that she was so intent on the things of God, and was so quiet and retired, that she would take no notice of their vagaries, and would consequently leave them to pursue their relaxed ways in peace. However this may be, Juliana had not long been prioress before her patience was exercised by these unworthy religious. The good sisters examined the conduct of their superioress, in order to imitate her virtues; but the others only to criticise, find fault, and murmur against her orders. The good rejoiced exceedingly at Juliana's wonderful and rapid progress in the ways of holiness, but the others interpreted everything she did in a bad sense, carped at everything, murmured at everything. Nor was this all; they were not content with murmuring in the convent, but spoke in the most disrespectful manner of their holy prioress, to all the seculars with whom they had an opportunity of conversing. These things being spread abroad, reports of the most exaggerated kind were soon in

circulation; since worldlings are always ready to
suspect things that do not exist, above all, when
persons consecrated to God are in question.

Juliana, who was ever watching over the in-
terests of those committed to her care, was not
long before she became aware of the disedifying
conduct of these unruly sisters. She endeavoured,
without delay, to bring them back to the regular
observance of their holy rule, but it was no easy
task. When it happens that religious have allowed
themselves to relax from their first fervour, and
fall into a life of tepidity and negligence, it
requires little short of a miracle to reform their
irregular conduct. It is only with the greatest
difficulty, and with the exercise of much prudence
and discretion, that this can be brought about;
even when it is the case with men, old habits and
old customs so cling to us, that it requires an
almost superhuman effort to shake them off. But
if it is so difficult to effect a reform in the case of
men, the case of women presents much more difficulty, since they are naturally self-willed and
obstinate. Juliana, in these trying circumstances,
acted as a wise and prudent superioress; she sought
first to lead them back to the ways of virtue by
sweetness, meekness, and charity, and by being
to them herself an example of every virtue. She
begged of them to be more reserved, to be more
discreet and circumspect in their conversations
with seculars; to love purity of heart, and to
prefer prayer and spiritual entertainments with
God, to the vain and frivolous conversations of
worldlings. But her charitable admonitions had
no effect on these unruly daughters; they spoke
only the more uncharitably and the more bitterly
against Juliana. Matters grew still worse, so that
at length the conduct of these religious, and what
they said against their mother, became the talk of

the city. The holy prioress was therefore compelled, in spite of her natural mildness and gentleness, to reprimand her rebellious subjects with greater severity : she told them plainly that such conduct, if persisted in, would inevitably lead to the worst of consequences; that, for the very honour of their sex, and their state of life, they should refrain from making themselves a scandal and derision to the whole city; or if they did not care for the opinion of men, they ought at least to fear God, and to bear in mind, that if He suffered them to continue in their evil courses for a time, He would, in the end, punish them for their iniquities, and with as much more severity as He had long and patiently awaited their amendment. But although compelled to warn them of their danger, and reprimand their faults with some severity, she nevertheless, in all things else, treated them with the greatest motherly kindness and affection, and endeavoured in every possible way to bring them to a sense of their duty. But whether she spoke to them mildly or severely, it was all the same ; they would neither observe the rule, nor would they refrain from their uncharitable manner of speaking of their superioress and the other sisters, whenever they could get an opportunity of conversing with seculars. Juliana was determined that at least one evil should be done away with, and that if she could not as yet bring them back to the observance of their holy rule, at least she would do all she could to prevent them giving scandal to the citizens. She therefore forbade them all communication with those outside the convent, and would not suffer them, under any pretext, to go to the parlours of the convent, as heretofore, and spend their time in useless conversations.

St. Benedict, in the chapter of his Rule in

which he speaks "of those who, though repeatedly
corrected, do not amend," thus speaks to the
abbot: "Hence, should he (the superior) find
that exhortation, the words of Sacred Scripture,
&c., fail to correct the delinquent, let him have
recourse to a yet more powerful remedy, that is to
say, his own prayers and those of the brotherhood,
that God, to whom nothing is impossible, may
vouchsafe to heal the infirm brother." This is
exactly what our Juliana did: she prayed day and
night for the amendment of the rebels, and also
procured the prayers of all the fervent sisters on
their behalf. Remembering the example of the
Good Shepherd, Who, having left His ninety-nine
sheep on the mountains, went to seek that which
was lost, and having found it, through compassion laid it upon His shoulders, and thus brought
it back to the fold: remembering this, she sought
by every means to bring back her wandering
sheep; warned them continually of their danger,
and called them to her, in tones the tenderness,
affection, and plaintiveness of which, might have
moved the hardest hearts. She watched over
them, frequently united them together, and exhorted them to the practice of virtue in the most
touching and moving manner. She never laid
her down to rest, without first ascertaining that
those for whom she feared were secure from every
danger. We may be sure that this solicitude for
the souls under her care was far from pleasing to
the arch-enemy of souls. If he could not, therefore, induce her by his artful suggestions to
become negligent in the duty of watching over her
daughters, he endeavoured at least to disturb the
rest and repose she so much needed after the many
and great labours of the day. She had scarcely
laid herself down to rest, after having assured
herself that everything was in proper order, than

this enemy of the human race would suggest to her that some of her daughters had departed from the convent; Juliana would then quickly rise, and search every part of the house, in order to assure herself that all her children were quite safe. This ruse of the devil was several times repeated, but Juliana was not long in ascertaining the cause of her disturbance. It may be that the devil acted in this manner in order to throw Juliana into an excited state of mind; and if he could have succeeded in this, he would then probably have assailed her with the contrary temptations of negligence 'in her duty, at a time when she would scarcely have been calm enough to resist him. Be this as it may, Juliana, by her prudence, overcame all the wiles and snares of the enemy.

The majority of the sisters, (who, as we have said before, were good and fervent,) were greatly edified by the care and attention Juliana so continually bestowed upon her subjects. Not so, however, the few relaxed ones. Their wounds were too old, and too inveterate, to be easily cured, especially since they refused to apply the remedies given them by their charitable physician. Instead of being grateful to their superioress for being kind enough to warn them of their danger, and endeavouring to preserve them from harm, they imagined that she had done them an injury; above all, they could not easily forget or forgive, her having forbade them those useless and frivolous conversations with worldlings, in which they had taken such great delight. To avenge themselves of the injuries they supposed they had received, they plotted and concerted together, upon the best means they could adopt to make the prioress feel the effects of what *they* considered her over-zealous and imprudent conduct. For

this purpose they no longer set bounds to their
malice and wickedness; and, in spite of the prohibition of Juliana, in spite of the scandal that
might be given by their conduct, they found some
means of communicating with the seculars, with
whom they had aforetime held so many frivolous
conversations, and, having persuaded them to
take their part against the prioress, they sought
by all possible means to destroy the good reputation Juliana had enjoyed hitherto with the citizens. Thus was a violent storm raised against
Juliana, both within and without the convent.
They spied all her actions, watched her as closely
as possible, endeavoured to throw discredit upon
her ecstasies and other favours which she received
from God; criticised all her orders, exhortations, pious admonitions, and everything she said
or did; but whatever malice they used, whatever
vigilance they might adopt in order to catch
unwarily their holy superioress, it was all in vain,
they could find nothing blameworthy in all her
conduct. This only maddened them the more;
instead of it opening their eyes to see the virtue
of Juliana, and their own wickedness, it made
them the more anxious to catch her in her words
or actions, in order that they might have where-
with to accuse her. But, seeing they prevailed
nothing, they at length had recourse to calumny:
they accused her of crimes of which she had never
so much as dreamed. But what did Juliana in
this case? She imitated her Divine Lord and
Spouse, Who, "when He was reviled, reviled not
again." She bore all these false accusations with
a constant and persevering meekness and patience;
she did not, however, discontinue any of her
efforts for the amendment of those who should
have been her true and loving daughters, but who
had become her bitter enemies. She prayed for

them unceasingly, putting her whole trust and confidence in God, who is able to grant the grace of conversion, even to the most wicked and rebellous. She continued to watch over the good order of the house, and both by word and example endeavoured to lead her children on to the perfection of every virtue.

In the midst of these troubles she had the consolation of seeing the majority of the sisters make rapid progress in the paths of holiness. The Prior of Cornillon, whose name was Godfrey, and whose house was very near to that of Juliana, also defended her against the false accusations and the unjust calumnies of which she was the object. He had ample opportunities of observing the conduct of Juliana, and being convinced that the evil which was said of her was false, he did all he could to preserve her reputation.

But Juliana's fervent prayers, her meekness, and her patience, were not all to be thrown away. God at length had pity on these religious; He graciously bent His ear to the supplications of Juliana and her sisters, and touched the hard hearts of those who had so long turned a deaf ear to His holy voice, calling upon them to repent and amend. What must have been the joy of our saint when she saw her wandering sheep return again to their faithful shepherdess, who had in so many endearing ways called them to her? What fervent thanksgivings would she not return to the bountiful and merciful Lord, who had shown so great mercy and pity to His unworthy creatures? All this can be better imagined than described. As for these religious themselves, we may reasonably hope that after their conversion they led lives so holy and so fervent, as to atone as far as possible for their former errors; and that thus they became to their holy prioress as much, and

6

more, a source of comfort and consolation than
they had before been a source of grief, pain, and
sorrow. Doubtless Juliana would incite them to
thank, bless, and praise God who had dealt so
mercifully with them ; and, in the words of the
Psalmist, would bless the Lord with them and for
them, saying, with all the fervour of which she
was capable, "Bless the Lord, O my soul, and
let all that is within me bless His Holy Name.
Bless the Lord, O my soul, and never forget all
that He hath done for thee. Who forgiveth all
thy iniquities : Who healeth all thy diseases:
Who redeemeth thy life from destruction : Who
crowneth thee with mercy and compassion. The
Lord is compassionate and merciful : long suffering and plenteous in mercy. He hath not dealt
with us according to our sins : nor rewarded us
according to our iniquities. For according to the
height of the heaven above the earth : He hath
strengthened His mercy towards them that fear
Him. As far as the East is from the West, so
far hath He removed our iniquities from us. As
a father hath compassion on his children, so hath
the Lord compassion on them that fear Him : for
He knoweth our frame. He remembereth that
we are dust. The mercy of the Lord is from
eternity and unto eternity upon them that fear
Him. Bless the Lord, all ye His angels : you
that are mighty in strength, and execute His
word, hearkening to the voice of His orders.
Bless the Lord, all ye His hosts : you ministers
of His that do His will. Bless the Lord, all His
works, in every place of His dominion, O my soul,
bless thou the Lord."*

* Psalm cii.

CHAPTER VII.

ST. JULIANA SOLICITS THE INSTITUTION OF THE FEAST OF CORPUS CHRISTI.

JULIANA had, therefore, at length, the consolation of beholding peace, regularity and fervour established in the whole house; she continued to rule her subjects well and wisely, and to be a model of every virtue to all. She was ever watchful and ever vigilant, knowing that she should one day have to give an account of her stewardship to that God Who judges with justice, and Who most certainly would examine strictly the manner in which she had governed and ruled the souls He had committed to her care. She, therefore, so acted in the performance of her duties, as that she might, at the last dread moment, hear from the lips of her Divine Spouse, the consoling words: "Well done, good and faithful servant; because thou hast been faithful over few things, I will set thee over many things; enter thou into the joy of thy Lord."

But, during all this time, she had never ceased to beg of Almighty God, to entrust some other person, (as *she* said more worthy,) with the task of soliciting the establishment of a new Feast, in honour of the Most Holy Sacrament of the Altar. She had not as yet spoken publicly of her vision, and the revelation she received concerning the establishment of the Feast; there was nothing she so much disliked as to do anything calculated to bring upon her the notice, much less the esteem of others. She never courted notoriety,

but most earnestly desired to be hidden and unknown.

Now, therefore, what was she to do? On the
one hand, she felt herself urged by God to procure the celebration of the Feast; but on the
other, she looked upon herself as unworthy, and
utterly incapable of accomplishing such an admirable project. Her devotion to the Blessed Sacrament was so great, that nothing could have given
her greater pleasure than to see it honoured with
a special Feast; but then she did not see how
she, a poor obscure nun, could accomplish so great
a work. Ah! who is there that ever can penetrate the designs of God? His ways are not as
ours, for, " as far as the heaven is from the earth,
so far are His thoughts above our thoughts."
Juliana, however, continued to beg of our Lord to
leave her in obscurity; she implored Him to confide the care of the establishment of so august a
solemnity to persons whose well known wisdom,
learning and authority, fully qualified them for
such an important office. She implored Almighty
God to be pleased to remember, that in His
Church there were many men capable of undertaking great affairs, and of accomplishing what
they undertook; but that she herself was a poor
weak woman, having no authority or strength for
such an undertaking; then she would say to our
Lord: " How, Lord, shall I commence this great
work? Having once commenced, how shall I
continue it? Having made some little progress
in it, how shall I bring it to a happy conclusion?
You, O dearest Lord, know my ignorance; how
then is it possible for me ever to succeed in such
an enterprise? Discharge me, I implore You,
from this heavy burden, and confide the care of
this thing to some one less unworthy."

But God did not hear our Saint in this matter,

however fervently she prayed; it was His Will that Juliana should have the honour of being the first to propose the Institution of the Feast of Corpus Christi; and that afterwards, persons illustrious both for piety and learning, should assist her in procuring it. However, Juliana, with that sense of her own unworthiness, which is the peculiar characteristic of all the saints, redoubled her fasts and prayers, in order that she might move God to discharge her from this important office. One day, when she had with more than ordinary fervour in prayer been showing forth her utter unworthiness for such a task, she heard a voice repeating distinctly these words of Holy Scripture: "I thank Thee, Father, Lord of heaven and earth, because Thou hast hidden these things from the wise and prudent, and hast revealed them to the little ones." Juliana knew then that she could no longer resist what was so evidently the Will of God, or if she did, how could she ever again sing these words of the Psalmist: "I have not hidden Thy justice within my heart; I have published Thy truth, and have not hidden Thy mercy"? She resolved, therefore, to execute the Will of God without further delay, since she was now persuaded, that He had chosen her for this work. Twenty years had now passed since she first had the vision, and during that time, how many prayers, sighs and tears had she not poured forth, in order to be released from the task? how many fastings, watchings and mortifications had she not employed for the same purpose? But, notwithstanding all this, now that she felt persuaded it was the Will of God that she should undertake it, she submitted herself to that ever wise, ever holy, ever adorable Will. Confiding in the help and assistance of God, she bravely undertook the work, and was resolved to accomplish it, whatever pain, trouble and anxiety it might cost her.

The first that she resolved to reveal the vision to, was her friend Eva, the recluse, and for this purpose she paid her a visit. After the first salutations were over, Juliana informed her friend that she had something to communicate to her; Eva begged of her to say whatever she pleased without restraint, assuring her that she would gladly share any pain or trouble with which she might be afflicted.

Juliana then said : "My dear Eva, I have for a long time been oppressed with a very heavy burden, and although, for many years, I have made great efforts to shake it off, it has not been possible for me to do so. I have never yet made the thing public, but since it is now necessary to do so, I have taken the opportunity of confiding it first to you. It is now twenty years since the globe of the moon, shining with great lustre, was presented to my gaze. This spectacle struck me with admiration; then I remarked that there was one dark spot which took away from it the perfection of its beauty. I was at first troubled by this vision; and as I feared some deception on the part of the malignant spirit, I endeavoured to banish the thing altogether from my mind. But whatever efforts I made, the vision was continually presented to my view, and followed me everywhere. I consulted some enlightened persons, and they counseled me to banish the thing from my mind; this, however, was impossible, so I prayed to be enlightened upon the subject. At length, God graciously heard me, and made me understand that the globe of the moon represented the Church of Jesus Christ; that the one dark spot, which hindered the perfection of its beauty, signified that one Feast was wanting; that this

Feast was one in honour of the Sacrament of the Altar, which God had determined should be instituted, and that He had chosen me to solicit its institution, I, who am only a vile slave, and incapable of succeeding in so important an affair."

We may imagine what it must have cost Juliana to have made such a declaration of the favour she had received from God; for nothing was more distasteful to Juliana than to be obliged to say or do anything calculated to make others think well of her; and well she knew that her friend Eva would esteem her, and think more of her than ever, after what she had just related. For this reason, it must have been painful for Juliana to speak of the favours she received from the Lord; but, however painful it might be, she had now, she believed, a duty to perform, and was resolved not to shrink from it at any cost.

As for Eva, what she had just heard gave her unbounded delight; she was filled with admiration of the designs of God, and praised, blessed, and glorified Him more than ever for having bestowed so many graces upon her friend. In order that she might the better be able to penetrate the mystery contained in this vision, she begged Juliana to obtain for her, from God, the same devotion that she herself had towards the holy Sacrament of the Eucharist. But the holy prioress refused her, and gave as her reason for doing so, that Eva's health and strength, which was already feeble and weak, would become entirely exhausted; for, she added, " whenever I meditate upon this adorable mystery, my strength becomes enfeebled, and nearly exhausted." Juliana, however, exhorted her friend to take courage, and assured her that the Infinite Goodness of God would grant her heavenly consolations in proportion to her strength, and that she would receive from them much peace and satisfaction.

Eva was not long in experiencing the truth of Juliana's words, for, in a very short time after, she was inflamed with such holy zeal, and animated with so great a desire for the new Feast, that she longed and desired, above all things, to see it instituted. But her ardent desires were mixed with many fears; for as she perceived many difficulties in the way, it was quite natural that she should have some doubts of seeing them all removed. She confided her doubts and fears to Juliana; but the latter, being full of confidence in the Almighty power of God, assured Eva that in the end the thing would be accomplished, and that most certainly the Feast would be established to the honour and glory of God, and for the benefit of His people.

But, although Juliana was resolved to accomplish the designs of God, as far as she was capable of doing so, she, nevertheless, was desirous that the honour of procuring the Feast should be given to another, rather than herself. For this purpose she looked around for some one to whom, in addition to Eva, she could reveal the whole mystery; unto whom she could entrust a part of the labour; whom she could animate with her zeal, and to whom, in the end, she could attribute the glory of success; for such was the modesty and humility of the holy prioress, that she wished for no honours of any kind to be given to her, nor any good attributed to her. About this time there lived at Huy, a religious of great sanctity, whose name was Isabella, whom Juliana thought would be just the person for her purpose. Isabella had, from her tenderest infancy, been making rapid progress in the way of perfection, loving, desiring and embracing labours, afflictions, crosses, and humiliations. She practised also, in great perfection, mortification of the body and of all the senses: her patience was so great, that she could endure the greatest injuries without manifesting the least resentment or impatience; her humility so profound, that she esteemed herself as nothingness, or rather as dust, ashes, sin and corruption; her charity so great, that she was ever ready to help and assist others, whatever pain or trouble it might cost her to do so; moreover, her love of God was so ardent, and her zeal for His honour and glory so great, that she seemed to set no bounds to herself, in anything connected with His love and service. Such a person seemed to Juliana admirably fitted for the object she had in view; but, in order to accomplish her design, it was necessary that they should have frequent conferences together, and if possible, live in the same house. Juliana, therefore, entered into negotiations, by means of which she obtained that Isabella should pass from Huy to the Convent of Cornillon.

Isabella, who had heard of the great virtue and sanctity of our Saint, was full of joy at the thought of becoming a daughter of so holy a mother. When everything was arranged, and Isabella had arrived at Cornillon, Juliana had long and frequent conversations with her on heavenly things, and was not long in ascertaining that Isabella, in all spiritual things, was very wise, learned and prudent. It sometimes happened that their discourses turned upon the extraordinary favours God sometimes bestows upon His most faithful and chosen servants; upon these occasions Juliana would address to her friend, searching, but prudent questions, in order to discover if God had revealed anything to her touching the Institution of the new Feast. Not discovering anything that could lead her to such a conclusion, she one day began to speak of the Holy Eucharist, and of the immense love to man displayed by God in this Holy Sacrament, and then said to Isabella: "Since we have, in this august sacrament, such an assured pledge of God's mercy, goodness and love to man, is it not right and proper that a special Feast should be instituted in its honour, and that this Feast should be observed by all Christians?" "For what end," replied Isabella, "since the Church *every* day celebrates these mysteries, and returns thanks to the Lord in the holy Sacrifice of the Mass? What do you wish more? If you desire that we should render the honours due to this holy mystery, the thing is impossible for us, since we are too weak and sinful to accomplish a thing so far above us. What comparison is there between the baseness and vileness of our nature and the Divine Majesty?"

An answer so unexpected took Juliana by surprise, and the pain she felt was as sharp as if a sword had suddenly pierced her heart; for if Isabella, whose zeal for God's honour and glory was so great, yet, nevertheless, received the idea of a new Feast in so cool a manner, what would others do whose indifference about the things of God caused them to receive everything connected with religion with coldness and indifference? But Juliana was not to be cast down at the first opposition, if opposition it could be called; she, therefore, had recourse to God, and begged of Him, Who is able to do all things, to change the opinion of Isabella, in order that she might co-operate with her in this great work. As for Isabella, she perceived that her answer had troubled Juliana, and since she knew that Juliana's devotion to the Blessed Sacrament was of an extraordinary kind, she began to suspect that Juliana had been

favoured by some revelation of which she was ignorant. She had always desired to have the same
sentiments of love and respect for the Holy Eucharist as Juliana had; but this made her more than
ever desirous to possess them, for this purpose
she was most fervent in her prayers to God, to
obtain from Him a greater devotion to the Holy
Eucharist.

About a year after this event, Isabella went one
day to visit the recluse of St. Martin's, and finding the doors of the church open, she entered to
pray. Devoutly kneeling before a crucifix, she
began her prayer; she had scarcely commenced
than she fell into an ecstasy, and contemplated in
her vision, heaven and all the celestial court.
She beheld in that moment all the different orders
of the heavenly spirits, prostrate at the foot of the
throne of Almighty God, begging Him to protect
the world, which was tending to ruin; to protect
the Church Militant, attacked on all sides by
heresies; imploring Him to employ the most efficacious means to cause the Faith to triumph,
since it was time now to manifest it. After having
heard this unanimous prayer of the blessed spirits,
a voice coming from the throne of the Divine
Majesty, declared that "their desires should be
accomplished, and that the Festival of the Most
Holy Sacrament, for which they had interceded,
should soon be celebrated by the Universal
Church."

As soon as Isabella had recovered her natural
state, she experienced an abundance of heavenly
consolation and sweetness, and an ardent desire
to see the Feast instituted without delay. Upon
her return to Cornillon, she related to Juliana the
vision she had been favoured with, and the effect
it had produced upon her. We may imagine
what must have been Juliana's joy when she

heard this glad news ; God had heard her prayer, and given her one who would assist her in the accomplishment of His Will, and to Him she returned most sincere and heartfelt thanks. Isabella, who at first was unable to see of what benefit the institution of the Feast would be, now that she had been enlightened by God, was so convinced that it was His Will, that she declared if all the world was opposed to it, she, nevertheless, would still continue, by every possible means, to endeavour to procure the establishment of this solemnity. .

Juliana and Isabella made a mutual compact to reveal to each other anything that God might further make known to them relative to the Institution of the Feast. They then consulted together as to the best means to adopt, in order to attain the aim of their desires. They resolved, therefore, to consult some learned men upon the subject, and, in the first place, they addressed themselves to John of Lausanne, a canon of St. Martin's, and a man of great learning and virtue, whom many persons eminent for erudition, sound doctrine and virtue, often consulted in their doubts and difficulties; and there were not a few who made it their glory and their boast, that they had received valuable instructions from this learned man. An anonymous but contemporary author calls him a man of admirable sanctity, " vir miræ sanctitatis," and, indeed, during the course of his life, he gave many proofs that the eulogium was well deserved. It was, then, to this man of God, that Juliana confided her revelations, and the orders she had received from God, relative to the Institution of the Feast of Corpus Christi. But the learned canon, although he had a very high opinion of Juliana's sanctity, was, notwithstanding, too wise and prudent to admit the truth of the vision without a careful examination; he never, for a second, had the shadow of a doubt about Juliana's veracity, but he knew that even the most holy are, so long as they are in this world, liable to error. He, therefore, examined most carefully and diligently by what spirit Juliana was led; but whatever care he took, he found nothing in her that could for one moment lead him to suppose any other thing, than that she was led by the Spirit of God. He was, in his own mind, quite convinced that the proposed Institution of the Feast, far from being opposed to the teaching of the Church, would, on the contrary, be a powerful means of exciting the faithful to greater devotion to that thrice-blessed Sacrament, in which Jesus hath given Himself to be our food. But Lausanne was of opinion that, before any further steps were taken in the matter, it would be well to see what the opinions of wise, learned and discreet men were, upon the subject. He communicated his thoughts to Juliana, and she begged of him to consult other theologians, without, however, mentioning her name in the matter, and after having consulted them, to please to relate to her their opinions upon it.

Lausanne most willingly undertook this commission; he consulted on the subject James Pantaleon, Archdeacon of Liège; Giles, John, Gerard, all three of the Dominican order, and celebrated for their learning and virtue: Hugh of St. Cher, the Provincial of the Dominicans, an order which has always been celebrated for being rich in good theologians; Guy, Bishop of Cambray, and the Chancellor of the University of Paris. These men, all well known for their wisdom, prudence, and learning, after a careful examination of the proposition made to them by John of Lausanne, unanimously declared that they found

that this Feast, far from being in opposition to the
dogmas of the Church, should, on the contrary,
be established, in order to excite and reanimate
the devotion of all Christians to the holy Sacrament of the Altar.

When Juliana, and her friends Eva and Isabella,
learned from Lausanne the favourable reception
which the proposition of the new Feast had met
with, from men so celebrated for their great
learning and piety, their hearts were so full of
joy and gladness, that it was impossible for them
to express it in words. They recognised that God
had done great things for them, since He alone
could have caused the proposition of a poor, weak
woman to be favourably received by men of such
weight and dignity. They therefore excited each
other to praise the Lord for His goodness, saying
to each other, in the words of the Psalmist: " O
magnify the Lord with me, and let us extol His
name together."*

CHAPTER VIII.

ST. JULIANA MEETS WITH MUCH OPPOSITION.

JULIANA having succeeded so far in the affair she
had so much at heart, was not so elated thereby as
to attribute anything to herself, but gave all the
glory to God. She was too grounded in true
humility to think for one moment that it was by
her own strength, or wisdom, or sagacity, or by
anything that she had said or done, that so
favourable a reception had been given to the idea

.* Psalm xxxiii. 4.

of the institution of the new Feast by men so celebrated. She simply desired the Feast to be celebrated, because she thought such to be the Will of God, and because she thought it would be for His honour and glory. She never for one moment thought that she would receive any honour by the institution of the Feast; hence it was, that whether things succeeded well or ill, she always preserved the same unalterable tranquillity; if she met with success, she was calm without any elation; if she met with opposition, she was serene and peaceful without the slightest perturbation. Nor was it in this matter only that she so acted; but in all affairs she undertook she was ever calm, patient, meek, and gentle; she did what it was her duty to do, and did it with the greatest possible perfection, leaving the successful or unsuccessful issue to God. Nor did it ever occur to her mind that if success attended her efforts, it was due to any virtue or effort of hers; with regard to the institution of the Feast of Corpus Christi, she never appears to have so much as suspected that Almighty God bestowed upon her the honour of being the first to solicit it, as a reward for her great devotion to the Blessed Sacrament. Yet when we consider how great her devotion to this holy mystery was, we may not unreasonably suppose that as a reward for this intense devotion, God honoured her with being the first to solicit a particular Feast in honour of this blessed mystery.

In all the works that Juliana undertook, she gave most evident proofs that she undertook them for the glory of God, and not through any motive of gaining the esteem or applause of men; since, whether men praised or blamed her, she always preserved the same evenness of soul, and when success attended her efforts, she gave all the glory to God, and acknowledged herself to be just what she and all of us are, dust and ashes. When we undertake any work or labour, we usually say, " O, my God, I desire to do this solely for Thy honour and glory." But, if it is so, as we say, how comes it that we are elated, if men praise us, and displeased and cast down if they speak against us ? If what we undertake is really undertaken for the honour and glory of God, how is it that we become angry at the least opposition, and full of impatience, fretfulness, and vexation, if things do not turn out as we wish ? Ah ! is it not because we have sought ourselves and our own honour, instead of seeking God and His honour and glory ? Is it not because we have humility on our lips, and but little of it in our hearts? Let us then firmly resolve from this moment to imitate St. Juliana in her profound humility, and in her purity of intention, so that whatever we do may be done for God ; and if our labours are crowned with success, let us attribute nothing to ourselves, but give to God all the glory. It is not permitted for us to desire the extraordinary graces bestowed upon Juliana, but we may, and we ought, to imitate her in practising those virtues which rendered her so pleasing in God's sight.

But to return to the history of our saint. After having learned from John of Lausanne the opinions of the other doctors, she thought it was now time to compose the Office for the new Feast. Knowing full well that God often makes use of simple souls to operate the greatest marvels, Juliana charged with the task of composing the Office a young monk of the monastery of Cornillon, whose name was John, and who afterwards became Prior of Cornillon. He at first was extremely unwilling to attempt such a work ; he therefore excused himself to Juliana in various ways, now

declaring his incapacity and want of talent, then
his ignorance of the works of the Holy Fathers.
But Juliana was determined that he should compose the Office, and the better to induce him to
undertake the work, she assured him that he
would receive from above, help, light, and assistance. Moreover, she promised to pray continually
for the success of his labours. John, who had a
high idea of the sanctity of Juliana, and the virtue
of her prayers, at length agreed to attempt the
task.

The young monk, whose many virtues caused
him to be beloved by all who knew him, spared
neither pains nor labours in the composition of
the Office; but while he was doing all that he
could to accomplish this task, Juliana was not
idle; she offered continual and most fervent
prayers to God for the success of his work. John
was not long in composing the Office, and when
completed, its style was so elegant and agreeable,
so beautiful and touching, that he himself said he
could not see anything at all of his own work in
any part of the Office, but confessed that all the
beauty, devotion, and piety there was in it, had
come from above. As each part of the work was
finished he submitted the revision of it to Juliana.
He knew that in all things connected with God
and His service she had great light and knowledge; therefore, if she thought any alteration
was needed, he corrected as she desired; if, on
the contrary, she judged no correction necessary,
he left it as it was. When Juliana had once
revised the work, he never afterwards made the
least alteration, but left it just as she had suggested.

Juliana had examined the work with such
scrupulous attention, and her judgment was so
sound, clear, and solid, that the great and learned

7

men to whom they submitted the Office to be corrected, saw nothing whatever that required alteration. On the contrary, they praised its beauty and its conformity to the teaching of the Church. Indeed, it appeared to them almost a miracle, that a young man of such moderate talents and learning should have been able to compose anything so beautiful. This Office, which commences with the words "Animarum cibus," was recited in the collegiate church of St. Martin, at Liège, until St. Thomas of Aquin composed his, a copy of which was sent by Pope Urban IV. to Eva the recluse; the chapter of St. Martin's then, according to the wish of the Pope, adopted the Office of the Angelic Doctor.

Another step had been taken in the affair Juliana had so much at heart, and again she had met with success: before, her solicitation for the new Feast had met with the approval of the learned and the good; now, the Office which had been composed was equally approved and praised. Those whom she had consulted were men distinguished for their learning and genius, men of authority, men well known for their zealous attachment to the Church, men whose morals and conduct in every respect were irreproachable. Juliana therefore thought, and with reason, that if these men approved of the design, she should, in the end, with their assistance, meet with success. She therefore begged of them, for the honour of God and the good of Christendom, to do all they could to procure the institution of this Feast, which they promised to do.

But now it was absolutely necessary that Juliana's vision should be publicly known, since, if the Feast was to be established, some reason for doing so must be given. The ecclesiastics to whom Juliana had spoken deemed it expedient to make known the reasons why the new Feast should be instituted, and who had been the cause of the project being first set in motion. They therefore spoke of the affair to their friends, and the latter, in their turn, spoke of it to others, so that in the city it soon became the news of the day.

. It was then that a violent storm was raised against Juliana, and that she had an opportunity of proving that her devotion was real, and neither feigned nor sentimental. Hers was not a thin, meagre piety, a religious sentimentality which cannot go beyond the beauty of taste or the pathos of a ceremonial, a devotion for clear, fine weather, but which cannot stand the storm. No; her devotion was real, and her humility sincere, so that amidst all the oppositions that were raised against her, she displayed heroic patience, unfailing meekness, and perfect tranquillity.

When the citizens of Liège first heard the news of the intended institution of a new Feast, the greater number of them were strenuously opposed to it. Some, who thought themselves moderate, said that at least it was extraordinary; others that it was an extravagance bordering on madness; some declared that Juliana's vision was a mere dream; others that it was the imagination of a weak brain, and an intellect deranged by excessive austerities. There were very few to be found who boldly declared it as their opinion that Juliana's vision came from God, and that the Feast should by all means be instituted. But it is consoling to find that those whose opinions, both on account of their learning and their attachment to the Church, were worthy of notice, were almost unanimously in favour of the institution of the new Feast; while, on the contrary, those who most bitterly opposed it, were, for the most part, people of depraved manners, and such as were a trouble and a scandal to all good Christians. There was a considerable number of good people who took no part whatever in the general discussion, but waited patiently until the Church herself had decided what was to be done in the matter.

Among the most ardent supporters of the institution of the new Feast, was Hugh of St. Cher, who declared that it would be of great utility to all Christian people, and a powerful means of obtaining the conversion of many souls to God. Not content with declaring this opinion in private, he ascended the pulpit, and maintained that it was most evidently the Will of God that a Feast in honour of the most Blessed Sacrament should be instituted, and that all opposition to it was vain and useless, since God would most assuredly accomplish His designs. His sermon, however, did not upon this occasion bring forth much fruit, but it was a seed which afterwards brought forth fruit a hundredfold.

It was not only from seculars that Juliana met with opposition, but ecclesiastics, and even some religious spoke against her, and made her the object of bitter and sarcastic railleries. But although they spoke so much against her, the only thing they could allege against the institution of the Feast, was the same that Isabella had already said to Juliana, when the latter first spoke of it to her, namely, that the Blessed Sacrament was sufficiently honoured in the daily Sacrifice of the Mass.

If Juliana met with so much opposition even from priests and religious, we need not be surprised to find the common people saying every evil against her. She soon became the subject of conversation upon every occasion, and in every place, in private houses, in taverns, in company, at feasts, in fine, everywhere she was the subject of debate, and the object of derision and scorn. Henriquez tells us that " it is almost incredible how many labours, persecutions and tribulations the blessed spouse of Christ had to undergo." They treated her as a visionary, some even as a hypocrite; and those who did not know her, spared no pains to vilify and calumniate her. She became the bye word of the whole city; they hooted at her, they hissed at her, they pointed at her the finger of scorn. Every day they fabricated new satires, each more offensive than the former; thus did she become the scorn and derision of all that dwelt around her.

Juliana, in the midst of this outburst of popular indignation, remained, as always, tranquil, meek, and gentle. It did not discourage her in the least; she was firmly persuaded that she was pleading the cause of God, and if she met with opposition it was no more than she might reasonably expect. For, if it was the work of God, and that there was a probability of its being useful for the salvation of souls, was it likely that the devil would remain idle? Would he not, on the contrary, use every endeavour to frustrate the work? Does he not always oppose everything calculated to give honour and glory to God? He is the enemy of all that is good, and consequently we always find that whenever any really good work is undertaken, he is sure, by his crafts, wiles, and arts, to seduce men to oppose it with the greatest vehemence and bitterness.

Our saint, however, in these trying circumstances, put her whole trust and confidence in God; she prayed without ceasing for her enemies; and, far from abandoning the good work, she became only the more zealous and the more ardent in soliciting the institution of the Feast of Corpus Christi. But it was not in Juliana's nature to act with precipitation; whatever her enemies might say against her, they could not, (at least with justice,) charge her with want of prudence. She who for twenty years had begged of God to be delivered from the office of soliciting the Feast, had no intention now of destroying the good work altogether by her imprudence or haste. She did not urge on the work, as if everything depended upon the speed with which it was to be accomplished. Nor, on the other hand, did she become careless and negligent; but, seeing that all her help, assistance, and succour must come from above, she determined to procure the intercession of the saints in heaven, knowing full well how powerful their prayers are with God. She had invoked their intercession before, but she now determined to do so in a still more solemn manner. For this purpose she undertook a pilgrimage to Cologne, that she might obtain the intercession of several martyrs, whose relics are deposited in the churches of this city. Our saint used every means in her power to perform this pilgrimage with the greatest possible devotion; and, after being fortified and strengthened with the Bread of Life, she commenced her journey. She took with her some of her sisters, who, without doubt, were at no loss to guess the motive of this pilgrimage. Having, after many labours and much fatigue, arrived at Cologne, she paid a visit to the church of the Prince of the Apostles, hoping to obtain his powerful intercession with God for the success of her enterprise. She prostrated herself before the high altar, and prayed with all the fervour of which she was capable. She was soon rapt in ecstasy, and remained in this state until the approach of evening: the sisters who accompanied her then endeavoured to bring her back to her natural state; they shook her, used every means they could think of, and at length carried her out of the church. When she returned to herself, she said to them : " Why did you arouse me ·before the harvest ?" We may gather from these few words the excess of delight she experienced in her raptures, since she would willingly and joyfully have remained so long a time in this state, without either seeking or caring for anything this world could bestow. Doubtless she experienced a foretaste of that overwhelming torrent of delights, which is the everlasting portion of the inhabitants of the realms of bliss. She visited upon the following days the other churches of the city, with the same piety and devotion, making in each long and fervent prayers, doing all she could to procure the help and intercession of the saints to whom the churches were dedicated, and of the martyrs whose relics reposed there.

But as the efficacy and power of the prayers of the greatest saint is not to be compared with the immense efficacy and power of the intercession of her who is the Queen of All Saints, Juliana determined to do all she could to procure the all-powerful prayers of Mary the Mother of God. She had always had a particular devotion to this good Mother ; but now, in her trouble and perplexity, she had more recourse to her than ever, because Mary is, and ever will be, " Consolatrix afflictorum," "Comforter of the afflicted." Before her return to Liège, therefore, Juliana made a pilgrimage to the Chapel of our Lady at Tongres. There are some who say that the Chapel of the Blessed Virgin at Tongres was built by St. Materne, and that it is the most ancient of all those built in honour of our Lady, north of the Alps. Whether this be really the case or not, we need not stay to inquire, since it has nothing whatever to do with our subject; be it as it may, it is certain that in Juliana's time it was a famous sanctuary of our Lady; the many favours Mary bestowed upon those who visited this shrine having made it widely known and greatly celebrated. We may well believe that Juliana's devotion in this holy place was easily awakened, and that she who had from earliest childhood tenderly loved our Lady, would, when bending before this holy shrine, with all the fervour of her soul, pour forth her prayers, tears, sighs and supplications to that dearest, best of Mothers, who is never invoked in vain. Nor can we for one moment suppose that Mary would allow so devout a client to depart without having received some consolation; especially since that client was suffering so much in her endeavours to procure a Feast in honour of that Sacrament, which Jesus, the Blessed Fruit of her womb, instituted the night before His Passion.

Juliana, having satisfied her devotion at this shrine of our Lady, afterwards visited the city of Maestricht, in order to implore the intercession of St. Servatius, whose body reposes in the noble collegiate church of this city. St. Servatius had been in his day a particular friend of St. Athanasius, and had given this holy bishop hospitality, when he was exiled from his country, on account of the persecutions of the Arians. St. Servatius had also been a most zealous, learned, and glorious defender of the Catholic doctrine of the Most Holy Trinity, in opposition to the heresy of Arius. Doubtless, Juliana thought, that one who had so zealously defended the truth, and so charitably assisted the persecuted in his lifetime, would not fail to be her protector in this her time of trouble, now that he enjoyed the Beatific Vision of God. She therefore implored the help of his intercession, with all possible earnestness and fervour.

After this, Juliana returned to Liège; but the enemies of the cause she had undertaken, or, to speak more correctly, the cause which God had requested her to undertake, still opposed her as obstinately as ever. They looked upon her pilgrimages as hypocrisy, and some of them even as mummery; her zeal for the establishment of the Feast of Corpus Christi, they declared was nothing else but the obstinacy of a woman, who took her dreams for revelations. Her humility, meekness, and patience, they said, were only feigned and apparent; and that she acted in this manner in order to gain the reputation of being a saint. But surely no Catholic will now say that Juliana's vision was a mere dream, or that her zeal for the institution of the Feast of Corpus Christi was obstinacy or pride; since the Church has approved both her vision and her zeal, by the institution of the Feast. Moreover, since its institution, all Catholics have had ample opportunities of witnessing the necessity for such a Feast. During the last three hundred years, how many blasphemies have there not been vomited forth against this thrice Holy Sacrament? And is it not right and just, that at least one solemn act of reparation should be yearly made, to atone for all these insults and blasphemies? Yes, most assuredly, we can say with the Council of Trent, that the celebration of this Feast, is "a pious and a religious custom." This venerable Council declares in its 6th Canon, that: "There has been established in the Church, the pious and religious custom of celebrating annually a Feast, to honour, with a special worship and solemn veneration, the great and ineffable Sacrament of the Eucharist; and that, from the same pious motive, the Blessed

Sacrament is carried in procession through the public streets and roads; it being very just that some days should be determined in which all Christians should testify their gratitude for the singular benefit they have received from our common Lord and Redeemer, in the institution of this mystery, which represents His triumph and His victory over death. It is also necessary that truth should triumph over falsehood and heresy, in order that the enemies of truth, at the sight of so great splendour, and in the midst of the immense joy which consoles the universal Church, should be smitten with pain and sorrow, and being covered with shame and confusion, should be converted." Moreover, the Council pronounces an anathema against those who declare this pious custom to be unlawful and sinful. "If any one shall say that Jesus Christ, the only-begotten Son of God, ought not to be adored with the worship of latria, nor externally adored in the holy Sacrament of the Eucharist; and that therefore it ought not to be honoured by the celebration of a particular Festival, nor be solemnly carried in processions, according to the praiseworthy and universal rite and custom of the Church; and that it ought not to be publicly exposed to the people that it may be adored, and that those who adore it are idolators, let him be anathema." "Siquis dixerit in sancto Eucharistiæ Sacramento, Christum unigenitum Dei Filium, non esse cultu latriæ, etiam externo adorandum; atque adeo nec festiva peculiari celebritate venerandum; neque in processionibus, secundum laudabilem et universalem Ecclesiæ nostræ ritum et consuetudinem, solemniter circumgestandum, vel non publice, ut adoretur, populo propenendum, et ejus adoratores esse idolatras, anathema sit."*

* Can. vi.

Certainly, then, bearing in mind the fact of the Church having instituted the Feast of Corpus Christi, and remembering also the great virtue and sanctity, the heroic patience and meekness, the perfect obedience, the sincere and profound humility of Juliana, we may well believe that her vision came from God, and that her zeal for the establishment of the Feast was neither pride, obstinacy, nor self-will ; but a true, real, earnest, and sincere desire for God's greater honour and glory. Let us then give most heartfelt thanks to the God of infinite love, Who hath raised up His servant to solicit and obtain the celebration of that joyous solemnity, in order to rejoice and gladden our hearts. In celebrating this Feast we may, if we will, catch at least a slight glimpse, even here below, of that glorious, everlasting, ecstatic worship, which is the eternal occupation of the blessed in heaven. In order that we may obtain a share of those graces, which are so abundantly bestowed on those who celebrate this feast devoutly ; let us, as each year brings round this gladdening solemnity, prepare ourselves to celebrate it with the greatest possible devotion. Let us prepare ourselves by fervent prayers, by frequenting the sacraments, and by every means that our holy religion offers. us ; and thus, by celebrating this solemnity with the greatest possible devotion, let us prove that we are grateful for the ineffable, inestimable treasure Jesus hath bequeathed to us, in giving Himself entirely to us in the sacrament of His love. Let us, not only upon the recurrence of this Feast, but also every day of our lives, thank Him for this unspeakable gift ; let us magnify Him because " He ruleth us, and we shall want nothing." Let us bless Him, because " He hath set us in a place of pasture, and hath brought us up on the water of refreshment." Let us extol His name for ever, because "He hath prepared a table for us against all them that afflict us."*

CHAPTER IX.

ST. JULIANA IS COMPELLED TO LEAVE CORNILLON.

THE struggle between Juliana's patience on the one hand, and the bitterness of her enemies on the other, still continued. But, however much her enemies might persecute her, or however violent the storm might rage, her patience was not to be overcome. The malice and bitterness of her enemies might be great; but her patience was still greater. She experienced everything that hatred, calumny, and malice could invent to discourage and humble her, but still her patience never failed. Such patience must necessarily, in the end, obtain the victory, or at least a temporary victory. People in whom there was still some remains of common sense, began to ask themselves if one who displayed such heroic patience could be as bad as she was represented to be? They then remembered the great reputation for sanctity our saint had formerly enjoyed, and then asked themselves what she had done to forfeit this good opinion? Nothing at all, except to solicit a Feast, in which, perhaps, after all, there could be no great harm. So, little by little they cooled down, and even changed their opinion altogether regarding the institution of the Feast; so that at last

* Psalm xxii.

the very persons who had been her most bitter opponents, were now the most zealous for the institution of the Feast.

But the spirit of prophecy with which God had endowed Juliana, forbade her to derive too much consolation from this temporary cessation of the storm. The tempest was to rage with more fury than ever, and through the instrumentality of one who ought to have been her most zealous and powerful defender and protector. She foresaw all this, and foretold it to her friend Eva, the recluse.

One day that Juliana was speaking to Eva about the institution of the Feast they both so ardently desired to see celebrated, Juliana said: "Although for several reasons there is some foundation for expecting some repose, yet I assure you I shall not be left in peace and tranquillity. They will declare against me a cruel war, and they will attack not only our holy mother the Church, but also all those who labour and are zealous in her defence. I assure you the arrows are already aimed at me, and that they will even commence to assail me this year, when Prior Godfrey is dead. He will have for his successor a man under whose government hell will rage with so much fury, that I shall be obliged to take flight. You will receive me, my dear Eva," she added, " with tears in your eyes."

But, during all this time, and in the midst of all the persecutions with which Juliana had been assailed, what part had the Bishop of Liège taken in the affair? The office of peacemaker, nothing more, nothing less. He had neither approved nor condemned the visions of Juliana; he had neither praised nor blamed the idea of the institution of the new Feast, but he had striven with all his power to preserve peace and harmony amongst his

flock. He held the virtues of Juliana in high
esteem, but he was far too prudent to give an
opinion hastily in a matter of so great importance.

The prophecy of Juliana relative to new troubles was unfortunately fulfilled to the very letter.
At the time Juliana had predicted, Godfrey, the
Prior of the monastery of Cornillon, died. He
was a good man, very zealous in the encouragement of virtue, and equally zealous to extirpate
vice; he had respected Juliana, and had used all
his power and influence to defend her character,
against the unjust slanders and calumnies of
which she had been a victim. In losing him,
Juliana had lost a great friend, and religion had
lost a zealous defender and protector.

The successor of Godfrey was quite a different
man: his name was Roger, and he obtained the
dignity of prior by unjust means; some writers
say that he purchased the dignity, and thus
rendered himself guilty of the sin of simony. He
was a man of dissolute manners, and an enemy of
virtue. He had an extreme aversion to Juliana;
whether the contrast of her virtue with his own
turpitude made him envious, or that Juliana,
knowing his wickedness, had given him some
advice, which, although salutary, was not pleasing,
we do not know; but certain it is, that from one
of these motives, or some other unknown cause,
he had an implacable hatred against our saint.
It might, however, simply be that Juliana stood
in the way of the execution of some one or other
of his wicked designs, which he soon began to
manifest.

Roger did not make use of his authority to
maintain regular discipline and good order in the
house confided to his care. On the contrary, he
sought, under various pretexts and shameful pre-

varications, to introduce irregularity and relaxation. Nor was he content merely to ruin the good order of his own house by his misrule, but sought also to bring ruin upon the good nuns who were thriving so well under the prudent government of their saintly prioress.

Under different and most unjust pretexts, Roger endeavoured to join robbery and theft, to the crime of simony, by which he had procured his dignity. He declared that the right of administering and managing the temporal affairs of the convent belonged to him. He therefore demanded Juliana to give up to him all the books in which were recorded the transactions of her house. But Juliana knew full well that if the management of the house was confided to him, everything would soon fall to ruin. If he was so acting, as inevitably to bring on the ruin of his own house, Juliana saw no reason why he should be allowed to ruin hers. She therefore assembled her daughters, and told them what the Prior wished to do; they unanimously agreed to oppose his designs, and resolved that they would not, under any pretext, yield to his unjust demands. This refusal irritated Roger beyond measure; his rage knew no bounds, and he resolved to avenge this (what he termed) insult of Juliana. He therefore associated with men as bad, and even worse, than himself, and made a compact with them to bring ruin upon our saint. These men, who had lost every sense of honour, and who were blackened with crime, were not at all unwilling to undertake the work.

Juliana's zeal for the institution of the Feast of Corpus Christi presented them with some foundation upon which to construct a popular tumult, which was to be principally directed against her. These men therefore dispersed themselves through the city, and declared, both publicly and privately, that large sums of money, which should have been distributed to the poor, and employed in other charitable purposes for the benefit of the citizens, had been given by Juliana to the bishop, in order to obtain the institution of a certain Feast. They moreover declared that they had manifest proof of what they alleged, since Juliana positively refused to render any account of the administration of the goods of her house to Roger the Prior of Cornillon, who had every right to know what was going on, and in what manner she discharged the temporal affairs of the convent.

Now, we have every reason to believe that if Roger had simply desired to inspect her accounts, Juliana, rather than have been the cause of discord, would have ceded to his demands. But the Prior of Cornillon aimed at nothing less than the entire administration of both houses, and this simply to have means of satisfying his unlimited extravagance. It is quite evident that Juliana and her sisters could never allow this; for, had they done so, they knew full well that he who was, by his misrule, bringing certain ruin upon his own house, would inevitably have drawn upon them the same misfortune.

But, unhappily, those to whom Roger's agents addressed themselves, could not see things in this light. It requires but little to excite the mob to acts of violence, and these men whom the Prior of Cornillon had employed, artfully suggested that Juliana had no right to be squandering large sums of money in endeavouring to procure the establishment of a Feast, which was a novelty, an innovation, and contrary to the wish of the people. They therefore gave it as their opinion that the accounts of the convent should be examined, and Juliana's unjust administration be made manifest.

Nothing more was needed to raise a sedition among the people; the very moment they thought their rights as citizens were infringed, they were ready for any acts of violence. They never stopped to consider whether the accusations against Juliana were true or false, but ran furiously to the convent. They entered with loud cries and expressions of rage, demanding to see the prioress; but the sisters, having been warned of what was going to happen, had secured Juliana in a place of safety, for they knew that the rage of the mob would be directed against the holy prioress. We have said above, in chapter three, that Sapientia had caused an oratory to be constructed, in which Juliana could give herself up to the exercises of prayer and contemplation. The mob, not being able to learn from the sisters where Juliana was, went to this oratory in hopes of finding her, but she was not there. They broke open the door and entered; then they forced open the chest in which the accounts were kept, and now God shows by a miracle that He approves of Juliana's refusal to submit the administration of affairs to Roger, and that she was in this guided by the Spirit of God. When the mob broke open the chest, the accounts were exposed to the manifest view of all, yet there was not one of the mob could see them. They had forced open the chest for the very purpose of finding the books: there they were, presented to the gaze of all, yet they could not see them. They were so manifestly visible, that nothing short of a miracle of the Divine protection could have hindered the mob from seeing them. Juliana concluded from this that she had done well in not confiding the administration of affairs to Roger.

The seditious mob, only the more enraged, in

8

proportion as the hope of finding the accounts of
the convent became less; cast themselves upon
two of the religious, who guarded the oratory,
overwhelmed them with injuries, and cruelly mal-
treated them.   Nor was this sufficient to satisfy
their malice; but they immediately proceeded to
the complete destruction of Juliana's oratory, in
which she had spent so many happy hours, and
received so many favours from God.   They broke
the tables, chairs, the bed, in fine, everything
that the oratory contained, they broke or tore in
pieces, and trampled under foot; nor did they
cease until they had completely destroyed and
razed to the ground, that little cell, which had
been the silent witness of Juliana's long and fervent prayers, her nightly vigils, her heroic mortifications, and the favours and graces God had
bestowed upon His servant in that hallowed sanctuary.

The wicked Roger, fearing lest the fury of the
populace should cool down, after the first burst of
its rage was over, and that all his plotting and
scheming would be frustrated, endeavoured to
gain the principal ones by bestowing upon them
rewards and presents, in which, unfortunately, he
succeeded only too well.   Thus, the tumult continually increasing, there was really some grounds
for fearing that there would be some lives lost
before the affair was terminated.

Juliana seeing this, believed it to be her duty
to abandon the house, in order that there might
be an end of this disgraceful sedition; she consulted her daughters, and they approved her design, promising to remain always faithful to her,
as their lawful superioress, and protested that
they would never abandon her.   Our Saint, therefore, without a single complaint, without a single
murmur against her enemies, voluntarily became

an exile from her own house, and taking with her
some of her daughters, went to beg a shelter from
the storm ; and a home was found for her, and
those she took with her, by Eva the recluse, who,
as Juliana had foretold, received them "with tears
in her eyes."

What a striking contrast is here presented to
us ! Juliana, all meekness, patience, gentleness,
mildness, forgiveness, charity ; Roger, full of
anger, envy, impatience, vexation, rage, revenge.
Both show us how important, how absolutely
necessary it is for us to mortify our passions. In
Juliana we behold an example of the happy results of this mortification, in Roger we see the
mournful consequences of its neglect. Juliana,
from her earliest childhood, had, with the assistance of Divine grace, laboured to mortify her passions, and thus had attained so great an empire
over herself, that whatever trials and persecutions
she had to endure, she ever remained calm, peaceful and tranquil. Roger, on the contrary, instead
of plucking up the bad weeds at their first appearance, had allowed them to take deep root ; and as
the more he neglected them, the more they spread,
they led him from one sin to another, from abyss
to abyss, until at length, he became so wicked, as
to raise a sedition, and urge on, (secretly, it is
true,) a riotous mob to deeds of violence against
a poor defenceless woman, who had never done
him the least injury.

It may be said by some : "But Juliana had
extraordinary graces, and having them, no wonder
she was so patient." It is quite true that she had
extraordinary graces, but we must also remember
that it is equally true she corresponded to grace.
We must not imagine, as some do, that the lives
of the saints are all sweetness and consolation.
Nothing could be further from the truth ; they

had to combat against their passions, and against the demon. They are not exempt from trials; on the contrary, they have sometimes to endure trials and temptations so great, that the mere mention of them makes us shudder. We have spoken briefly, in a previous chapter, of some of the trials Juliana had to pass through, and how, by the help of Divine grace, she came out of the conflict, glorious and victorious. We learn, then, from the example of our Saint, that if we seek to mortify our passions, we must be prepared for a combat, not only with nature, but also with the devil, who is sure to allow us no peace, when once we begin in earnest the practice of this necessary mortification. But if it is, without doubt, hard and difficult to undertake this mortification, yet its reward is exceeding great, and the consequences of its neglect terrible, as we see in the example of Roger. If we neglect to mortify our passions, we may fall as deep, and deeper, than he did. More-over, we must remember that in this struggle, God is ever ready to give us His grace, in order that we may conquer, if only we ask it of Him in the right way. We have also examples of the heroic courage displayed by innumerable saints, to spur us on, and to animate us in the strife. Juliana is not the only example of a saint who had thus to struggle and fight, all the saints have had to combat either their own passions, or the devil, or both.

The great Apostle St. Paul, who was "rapt even to the third heaven, caught up into Paradise, and heard secret words, which it is not granted to man to utter;" even he was not exempt from this spiritual combat, for he says of himself: "Lest the greatness of the revelation should lift me up, there was given me a sting of my flesh, an angel of Satan to buffet me."* And if this glorious apostle was not free from trials, can we expect our passions to be extinguished without any pain or trouble? Assuredly no; we cannot.

Again, what long, terrible struggles, against both the demon and their passions, many of the ancient Fathers of the Desert had to suffer, yet they wearied not of the strife; but struggled on and on, until they gained the victory.

As long, then, as our passions remain altogether unmortified, we must not attribute this immortification so much to our natural disposition, as to our indolence in eradicating the pernicious weeds, through which they have grown now to such an extent, that it requires an immense amount of patience and perseverance to root them out.

The saints had to struggle against their natural dispositions, and so must we. St. Ignatius Loyola was of an ardent, fiery disposition, and yet, from the effects of his combats against nature, he had so perfectly subdued his natural temperament, that those who did not know the reality of his character, would have believed him to be of a phlegmatic temperament.

St. Francis of Sales was naturally bilious and choleric, but by the violence he offered himself, he became the gentlest of men, and a model of meekness.

St. Vincent of Paul was by no means one of those phlegmatic persons whom nothing could move; on the contrary, he was ardent, lively, quick, full of fire; yet, by his continual combats against nature, he became the mildest of men.

But we should never end if we were to relate all the examples of the saints, who have overcome their natural dispositions. The life of Sister

* II. Cor. xii.

Frances of the Blessed Sacrament, however, presents us with such an interesting example of a
long continued and heroic combat with the passions, that we cannot refrain from quoting it.
Her life has been written by M. B. De Lanura,
and he tells us, that she was naturally of an im-
petuous disposition, savage and fiery as an Afri-
can.   At the age of seventeen, she had formed a
criminal connexion with a young man of her
family, and nothing less than a miraculous apparition was necessary to draw her from this
abyss.   One day, it seemed to her that she saw
the earth open under her feet, and she gazed with
indescribable terror upon hell, yawning beneath
her.   She immediately entered the convent of
discalced Carmelites at Soria, made a general
confession, and commenced her noviciate.   But
she had to endure a terrible struggle against her
own nature and against the demons, who sought
to drive her to despair, by the remembrance of her
past sins ; she was, however, consoled from time
to time by other visions, and coming off victorious
in this combat, she made her profession.   New
struggles, and still more terrible, awaited her.
She was naturally impatient, and easily moved to
anger.   The least wrong that was done to her,
rendered her spiteful and jealous, and to look at
her the wrong way, was sufficient to excite her
anger.   This disposition drew upon her frequent
penances ; but, in spite of her good resolutions,
she was continually falling.   All her other passions had the same character of impetuosity.   Her
senses were unmanageable ; she could neither re-
collect herself, nor taste spiritual consolations.
But she resolved to struggle until she obtained
the victory.   For this purpose, she spared neither
pains nor labour ; she prayed continually, she
fasted, she practised every kind of mortification,

she tore her flesh with long and cruel disciplines, she girded herself with cilices; nothing was neglected, no means left untried, in order to obtain the victory. The Lord one day appeared to her, and said: "Thou complainest to Me, and forcest thyself to walk in My presence; but thou shalt not obtain this by violence and force. Walk before Me in sweetness and a good conscience, and thou shalt be solaced." Indeed, the excessive mortifications to which she had condemned herself, could scarcely break her nature, against which she had to struggle, even to her old age.

She seems also to have been incapable of drawing any one to sympathize with her, so that she could not obtain the least consolation, or the least encouragement, to sustain her in her many trials. She spoke in a disagreeable manner, and her countenance, her bearing, her gait, her whole comportment had something in it repulsive, so that every one avoided her. At nearly every chapter she was severely punished by her superiors; she was reprimanded by her confessors, and accused by her own conscience. But she never excused herself; she complained to God alone in prayers and tears. God, one day, said to her: "I wish thee to struggle against thy natural disposition; do not weep, therefore, but correct thyself." When she was upon the point of giving way to the violence of her temper, our Lord would appear to her with an angry countenance, and reprimand her severely. The Provincial having come to visit the convent, the sisters, as if they had been moved to do so by an evil spirit, all began to accuse her. She received a severe reprimand, and was condemned to seven months penance, separated, during three months, from the community, and deprived of the Holy Communion. Three times in succession, at the

visit of the Provincial, this trial was renewed.
Plunged in the profoundest desolation, she, however, did not lose her calmness and resignation,
although she was, besides this, troubled by the
demons, who ceased not to appear to her, and
torment her, even until the last four years of her
life. In addition to all this, the flames of concu-
piscence were enkindled in her with incredible
violence; every member of her body seemed to be
burning with the fire of hell. This state lasted
until she was sixty-two years of age; and the
temptations with which she was besieged, ceased
only after a struggle of forty-six years, a few days
before her death, which happened in 1629, in the
sixty-eighth year of her age.

Surely the bright examples of these deeds of
heroism are sufficient to make us resolve to begin,
this very moment, the practice of the mortification of our passions. If we have neglected this
necessary mortification hitherto, let us now begin.
If the struggle should be long and painful, let us
not despair; the reward of perseverance surpasses
all that we can think or conceive. If a long
series of years should pass away before the accomplishment of the task, let us not grow weary of
the strife : "For in due time we shall reap; if we
faint not." No matter what opposition, no matter what obstacles we meet with, let us never give
up the struggle. When faint and weary, and
exhausted with the labour of the combat, let us
seek strength and refreshment, where alone it is
to be found; where Juliana and all the saints
have found it; in God. "They cried to the Lord
in their affliction, and He delivered them out of
their distress."* Let us also, in imitation of
Juliana and all the saints, call upon the Refuge

* Psalm cvi. 13.

of the miserable and afflicted, Mary the Queen of Heaven; for this sweet Mother is never invoked in vain. But there is yet another source of Life and Strength, to which, during their combats, Juliana and all the saints frequently had recourse; and that is, to the life-giving Sacrament of the Eucharist. If, then, our combats are furious and prolonged, let us the more frequently fortify ourselves with this heavenly manna, for it will give us such life and strength and vigour, (if duly received,) that we shall be enabled to continue our journey, until we come to that place of joy and blissful rest, where we shall "sing the mercies of the Lord for ever and ever."*

CHAPTER X.

ST. JULIANA'S LIFE AT ST. MARTIN'S.——HER CHARITY TOWARDS HER ENEMIES.——HER RETURN TO COR-NILLON.

THEY only who have been forced to leave the home of their childhood, can give an idea of what it must have cost Juliana to quit Cornillon. How frequently do exiles from their home call to mind the many well-beloved spots, which bring to their memory affectionate remembrances of the sweet and happy days of yore? Juliana had spent all her life in the Convent of Cornillon, her earliest remembrances and affections were bound up with the dear old place. But, besides the natural ties that make the home of our childhood so dear to

* Psalm lxxxviii. 1.

us, there was, in Juliana's case, other things that rendered the Convent of Cornillon doubly dear to her. It was here, that she had dedicated herself to the service of God, in pronouncing the religious vows, which bound her to Him for ever, and made her His spouse. It was in this place that she had learned to triumph over the world, the flesh, and the devil. Here it was, that she had received so many celestial favours, and such an abundance of Divine grace. How dear, then, must this old convent have been to her! How keenly she must have felt her exile from its much-loved walls, which had so long sheltered her, and preserved her from the many perils and dangers of this deluding and deluded world! But, keenly as she must have felt the separation, she was so resigned to the Will of God, that she departed without a murmur.

Then, again, the circumstances under which she was compelled to leave, made the exile doubly painful. She was not compelled by poverty to seek an asylum elsewhere, but was driven out through the evil machinations of one who should have been her friend and brother. Had she been driven out by a foreign enemy, it would not have been so difficult to bear; but the enemy who drove her away was not a foreign, but a domestic one. There was also another source of trouble; she could not take all the sisters with her to St. Martin's, because Eva could not find room for all. In this case, what was to become of those she left behind? Would they remain faithful in the observance of their holy rule, or would they fall away? It is true they had promised to remain faithful to her, but would they? All this she must leave to God. He had permitted the thing to happen, and she was resigned to His ever adorable Will. And so, without the least manifesta-

tion of impatience, without the slightest murmur
or complaint, she departed, leaving the future in
the hands of Him, who knows how to bring good
out of evil. Thus it was that she showed more
by her actions, than by her words, that she was
perfectly detached from everything.

Upon the arrival of Juliana and her sisters at
St. Martin's, Eva, though weeping bitterly over
the things that had happened, nevertheless received them with the tenderest marks of affection.
Eva was deeply afflicted to see her good mother
reduced to so sad a condition, but they consoled
each other as well as they were able, and adored
the decrees of Divine Providence. The recluse
did all she could to furnish what was necessary
for her guests, but as she was herself only a poor
recluse, we may be sure that their poverty was
very great. But however great it might be,
they were deeply and doubly grateful to the
holy recluse, for her good will in doing all she
could to solace them in their affliction. These
blessed servants of the Lord, however, cared little
for the things of this world; it was God they
sought, and they could find Him as well at St.
Martin's, in great poverty, as they could at Cornillon, where their little wants had been accustomed to be charitably ministered unto, with tenderest care, by Juliana. Their conversations in
this little retreat were all upon God and spiritual
things. They frequently spoke of the necessity
of remaining faithful to God in adverse, as well as
in prosperous affairs; of the happiness to be found
in the service of God, and of the fragility of all
human things. These conversations on spiritual
subjects were followed by reading aloud, and by
prayer, in which latter exercise they spent a good
part of the night.

But God, Who never forsakes those who do not

forsake Him, raised up a friend for His persecuted servants. The exact number of the sisters who went with Juliana to St. Martin's is not known; but, however few or many they might be, it is certain that this little retreat was too small for them to perform their religious exercises with that decorum, that religious consecrated to God are accustomed to. But the friend whom God raised up, now appears in the person of the Canon John of Lausanne, whom, it will be remembered, Juliana had consulted about the institution of the Feast. He, touched with compassion at seeing them thus exiled from their happy home, begged them to occupy his house, which was larger and more commodious for the performance of the duties of the religious life, than the one they at present occupied. But he was not content merely to give them a shelter; he also, with great generosity, offered them the half of his income. It must have been very consoling to Juliana, to have met with such a friend, at the time she so much needed one. She testified the most sincere gratitude to her benefactor, and, together with her sisters, blessed and praised the goodness and mercy of God, Who had touched the heart of the good canon, and inspired him with so much compassion and charity for His servants.

The charity of John of Lausanné did not end even here; he was firmly convinced of the injustice of the accusations which had been brought against Juliana, and as he was an ardent lover of justice, he determined to use all his influence and power to bring back the exiles to their home. He defended the character of Juliana against her unjust accusers, both publicly and privately. He consulted upon the best steps to be taken in the affair, with the Bishop of Liège, whose name was Robert, and who highly esteemed the virtues and sanctity of Juliana. This bishop was celebrated for his learning, zeal, and piety; he had a particular esteem and love for all those who were known to be virtuous and holy. He, during his episcopate, dedicated several churches, repressed a great many abuses, re-established regular discipline in many monasteries, and gave all his care and attention to make his clergy live according to the rule and maxims of the Gospel.

Such a man as this was sure to lend a willing ear to John of Lausanne, when he demanded justice to be done to these poor persecuted women. But, even before John of Lausanne had spoken to him, the bishop had firmly resolved that justice should be done. Before, however, any steps could be taken, it was necessary for the bishop to see Juliana, and hear from her own lips the particulars of this scandalous affair. The bishop, therefore, went to St. Martin's, and saw Juliana, but not one word of complaint or murmuring against her enemies passed her lips. The bishop was greatly edified at such conduct on the part of one who had been so deeply injured; he, therefore, consoled our Saint in her afflictions, gave her his benediction, and departed.

But if Juliana was disposed to suffer in silence, it was not the intention of the bishop that so flagrant an ·act of injustice should remain unpunished. If Juliana's charity could forgive all, the bishop's sense of justice would not permit him to leave her undefended. He and Lausanne, therefore, came to the conclusion that they were bound in common justice to institute a process against the prior. In order to succeed, they set about examining the whole conduct of the wicked prior, and as they were very zealous in the work, they were not long in discovering abundant proofs of his bad conduct, and irregular manner of living.

But while the bishop and John of Lausanne
were labouring with all their power for the justifi-
cation of Juliana's character, those who favoured
Roger, and those whom Roger employed, spread
abroad all manner of evil reports of our Saint.
They accused her of having acted contrary to her
rule, of having introduced novelties and irregularities, of having imposed upon the people by her
pretended visions and revelations; they accused
her of harshness to her subjects, of having most
unjustly attacked the unsullied reputation of the
prior; in fine, they invented against her a thousand calumnies and unjust accusations. These
false reports at length reached the ears of Juliana; but our Saint never manifested the least
resentment or impatience against her enemies.
She did not even seek to justify herself, nor did
she say one word to lead others to believe that
she was any better than her enemies described
her. She most literally fulfilled the Gospel
precept: "If any one smite thee on the one
cheek, turn to him the other also." For as her
enemies smote her with one accusation, she, by
her silence and forbearance, gave them ample
opportunity of smiting her with another. But
she was not merely forbearing, meek, patient and
gentle, she also loved her enemies, and shewed
her charity by praying unceasingly for them.

The bishop and John of Lausanne, having
accumulated abundant evidence of the wickedness
of Roger, and having their witnesses in readiness,
brought the affair before the proper judges. The
Prior Roger was accused of simony, of destroying
monastic discipline, of squandering the goods of
his monastery, of persecuting Juliana, and of
secretly urging on the people to seditious and
riotous acts of violence, in order to force her to
leave her house.

Juliana was now obliged to speak, but she was deeply grieved that this should be the case. Now was the time to manifest her real charity; she had now full opportunity of speaking against her enemy, and of showing up his disgraceful conduct in its true light. But far from wishing to say anything to injure her enemy, she was ready to defend his honour, and it was to her a real cause of grief to see him in this painful situation. She was compelled by her conscience to adhere strictly to the truth, but she nevertheless alleged every motive she could think of that might in any way palliate his wicked conduct.

These generous sentiments of our saint greatly edified the judges; but, fortunately for the cause of justice, Juliana was not the only witness. Reliable and trustworthy witnesses were brought forward, who proved beyond all doubt that Roger had been guilty of simony in obtaining the dignity of prior. Other witnesses were brought forward to prove, that the prior was the real main-spring of the riot in the city. The monks of his own monastery were then sworn, and their declarations proved that he had introduced many relaxations and irregularities in the priory, and that he had entirely subverted monastic discipline. The nuns were then sworn, and they gave evidence of the injuries that had been done to the two religious who guarded Juliana's oratory, and of the entire destruction of the oratory itself; all which was to be attributed, at least indirectly, to Roger, since, as had been proved, he was the real main-spring and prime-mover of the sedition. But there was one witness of more importance than all the rest, who of his own free-will came forward. This was a confidential servant of the prior, who, touched with repentance of the excesses he had committed with his master, cast himself at the feet of the judges and declared the truth of the whole affair. He, moreover, declared that the manner in which the prior had squandered the goods of the priory was excessive in the extreme, and that Roger's extravagance was unbounded and unlimited. The accusations that had been circulated in the city respecting Juliana, were found, upon examination, to be destitute of even the least appearance of truth, and to have been invented solely and only by the malice of her enemies.

All the witnesses in the case having at length been heard, the judges proceeded to give sentence. They declared Juliana to be entirely innocent of the things which had been laid to her charge, and they re-established her with honour as prioress of her convent. They then declared Roger to have been guilty of simony in procuring the dignity of prior, and as he was not lawfully prior, they deposed him. They also found him guilty of raising a sedition in the city, and of the other things laid to his charge, and, having imposed suitable penances upon him, they sent him to a monastery of his Order situated near the city of Huy.

The innocence, virtue, and sanctity of Juliana having been so clearly and so publicly demonstrated, people began to venerate and respect her more than ever. Her enemies had thought to annihilate her and render her odious in the sight of all the people; but their bitter persecutions had only enhanced her reputation. No signs of triumph over her enemies were visible in Juliana; she was still the same meek, quiet, gentle woman she had ever been, and was quite ready to lay down her life, if necessary, for those who had persecuted and calumniated her.

The bishop wished to rebuild at his own expense the oratory which the seditious mob had destroyed, and was going to place it in a more healthy situation. But John of Lausanne and Eva were anxious that it should be built upon the same spot as before, and the bishop yielded to their desires; we can well believe that Juliana appreciated this proof of the affection of her friends.

During Juliana's exile from Cornillon, affairs at the monastery had been even worse than before, and now that Roger was deposed, it became necessary to choose one to fill his place; but it was absolutely requisite that the one chosen, should be able to restore the primitive fervour and discipline of the house, and repair the evils that had been brought in by Roger. But those who were capable of undertaking the office, fearing new troubles, were unwilling to do so. Those who were not capable of governing well, having neither the requisite virtues, nor talent, were nevertheless desirous to obtain the dignity. There was no sort of rule now being observed in the monastery : it was in a sad state; everybody wished to govern, and nobody was willing to obey. In this state of affairs there was every reason to believe that troubles would recommence, and that finally it would result in the entire ruin of the house.

Juliana, who loved her Order, was most anxious to avert such a calamity; accordingly, she had recourse to God, Who was always her refuge in time of trouble. She knew that He would listen to her cry, hear her prayer, and enlighten her as to the best course to be pursued. She was not content with praying herself, but she also caused all her daughters to pray fervently for a happy termination to this sad state of affairs.

Not merely did she assist in the work by her prayers, she also used all her influence to procure the election of an active, vigilant, and zealous superior, for she knew that such a one was abso-

9

lutely necessary to repair the many existing evils. She foresaw the tempest which would arise against whoever had this office, and on this account was at first rather unwilling that this post should fall to the lot of the young monk John, who had composed the Office of the Blessed Sacrament. However, when she reflected upon his virtue and talents; that none were more capable of restoring monastic discipline ; none more able to rule the house well and wisely than he, in regard both of spiritual and temporal things, she resolved to use all her influence to procure his election. In fine, by her fervent prayers, and by the use she made of whatever influence she possessed, her desires were accomplished, and John was elected prior.

Peace once more being restored, Juliana began to resume her former manner of life. She had wished to remain hidden and unknown ; but, after having been brought so prominently before the public, and her great virtue so clearly manifested, retreat and seclusion were henceforth impossible. Everybody now sought to know her ; her patience, her meekness, her fortitude, and her courage, were everywhere, and by everybody, spoken of. She was revered and venerated by all as a saint. Even the ecclesiastics who had formerly mistrusted her visions, and attributed them to every cause but the right one, now began to honour her, to speak of her in the highest terms of praise, and to defend her both publicly and privately. Besides the air of sanctity which her close and intimate union with God gave her, there was in her whole person something angelic and supernatural, which drew all who conversed with her to form the most favourable impressions of her. Her modesty and simplicity showed the angelic purity of her soul; her gestures and actions were so measured and so composed, that a great man said of her: "During the thirty years I have known her, I have never once seen her move her body without necessity." Her movements were neither too precipitate nor too slow, but grave and moderate; in fine, her whole exterior was such as to call forth the admiration and veneration of all who saw her. She was, moreover, naturally eloquent, and spoke with ease, grace, and wisdom, even upon ordinary subjects; but when she spoke of God, her natural eloquence rose even to sublimity, so that she carried away, and as if by force, the hearts of all who listened to her.

Seeing that she was endowed with such rare qualities, we need not be surprised to find that many were desirous of making her acquaintance. Not only the poor, the needy, and the unlearned, sought her; but even men celebrated for their wisdom, talents, and learning, considered it a great privilege to be allowed to converse with her; and it has been avowed that such was the wisdom with which she spoke, that many have learned more of the mysteries of faith in conversing with Juliana, than they were able to learn otherwise by long and serious study. Such was the good odour that Juliana spread around her, that through her the convent of Cornillon was held in high esteem by all lovers of truth and virtue.

Although frequently called upon to converse with creatures, she never for one moment lost that close and intimate union with God, Who was the One, Supreme, and only end of all her affections and desires. Neither did the esteem and veneration in which she was held, ever for one moment extol her, or cause her to think anything of herself; on the contrary, she thought herself the most unworthy, the last, the least, the lowest of all. As in the midst of adversity she was always resigned to the Will of God, and always remained mistress of her passions; so in prosperity she was not high-minded, but humble, simple, meek, and lowly. If her humility would have permitted her to speak of herself, she could with truth have said with the Royal Psalmist: "Lord, my heart is not exalted, nor are my eyes lofty. Neither have I walked in great matters, nor in wonderful things above me."*

CHAPTER XI.

ROBERT, BISHOP OF LIEGE, INSTITUTES IN HIS DIOCESE THE FEAST OF CORPUS CHRISTI.

Notwithstanding all the oppositions that Juliana had met with, her zeal for the institution of the Feast of Corpus Christi had never relaxed. She was intimately persuaded that the establishment of the Feast was God's Will, and consequently she never wearied in labouring for its institution. Many ecclesiastics of great learning and high dignity, and many laymen of noble birth, drawn by her reputation for sanctity, came to visit her and beg the assistance of her prayers. She used all her eloquence with them to induce them to advance as much as possible the great work she had so much at heart. As several doctors well known for their piety and learning, had already sanctioned her design, and declared it in strict conformity with Catholic doctrine, no wonder the others she spoke to upon the subject were of the same opinion, and promised to do all

* Psalm cxxx. 1, 2.

they could to further the good cause. But, besides her eloquent arguments, there was another much more powerful reason which inclined men to give heed to her project, and that was her extraordinary and well-known sanctity; her patience and courage in adversities; her great charity towards her enemies. It was these virtues, more than anything else, which gave weight to her revelations. They saw manifested in her, a power for good works such as God alone could give, and from this they concluded that her visions, which had been so much disputed, must have come from God.

Among those who visited Juliana frequently, were Robert, Bishop of Liège, and Guy, Bishop of Cambrai, both prelates of great reputation, and their constant visits augmented still more the reputation of our saint. Juliana, suspecting that Eva the recluse had something to do with the reputation she was acquiring, reproached her with it, and begged her never to say anything that could draw upon her the esteem of the great. Juliana also declared to her friend that she had begged from God that He would bestow upon her before her death the favour of being persecuted, as much as she was now being honoured and respected. We shall soon see that God had respect to her and heard her petition.

Although the Bishop of Liège frequently visited our saint, and although he was often solicited by many learned men to institute in his diocese the Feast of Corpus Christi, who assured him also that it would certainly be productive of good results; he, nevertheless, always replied: "We cannot rashly institute a new Feast upon the mere visions of a woman." But although the Bishop spoke in this manner, he continued to visit Juliana. She often spoke to him of the institution of the new Feast, and used all her eloquence to persuade him to have it celebrated in his diocese ; but, for the present, her arguments were all in vain. No matter how vividly she painted the glory that would be given to God by the institution of this Feast, no matter how eloquently she described the comfort, consolation, and graces the faithful would receive from its celebration, the Bishop was deaf to all. Juliana foretold to him several things, the truth of which he afterwards experienced ; but even this did not convince him of the truth of her vision : he never doubted her veracity for one moment ; but he was an exceedingly prudent man, and one who feared, above all things, the visions and revelations of women. He mistrusted these things in women, perhaps, because he had an extreme idea of their weakness, and because experience has shown that they are much more liable than men, to be deceived in such matters.

It may, however, seem strange to some, that the bishop should think and speak so highly of Juliana, should publish everywhere her great virtues, should relate her sayings as so many oracles, and yet have so much reluctance to insti- tute a Feast, which he knew was not at all contrary to the doctrines and teachings of the Church, although earnestly solicited to do so by her whom he esteemed so highly. But, if we reflect a little, we shall recognize in this the guiding hand of an All-Wise Providence. It was God's work, not man's ; and in order to show more clearly that it was His work, He permitted it to be opposed, and to be opposed, moreover, by the very one in whom, humanly speaking, all hopes of success in the work were placed. For if the bishop refused to take the thing into consideration, it was not at all probable that other ecclesiastics of any dignity or authority in the Church would listen to the proposition. If, in this matter Juliana's own bishop took her for a visionary, would not every other bishop come to the conclusion that he had good reasons for doing so? In this case they also would refuse to listen to the proposition, and then nothing could be done in the matter. Now, none but God, could convince a man so extremely unwilling to believe in the truth of the vision as the bishop. If the design was of God, God would sooner or later convince him that it was so; if it was not of God, then the thing would come to nought. God, therefore, permitted the bishop to doubt, in order that afterwards it might more clearly appear that the institution of the Feast was really the Will of God, since, in spite of the conscientious opposition of the bishop; in spite of the enraged opposition of the demon; in fine, in spite of every obstacle that was raised, He Who is all-powerful and is able to accomplish what He wills, did in the end bring the work to a happy conclusion, but in such a manner that none could with any reason doubt it to be His work.

We might reasonably have expected that this long and persevering opposition of the bishop would have cooled the ardour and zeal Juliana had hitherto displayed for the institution of the Feast. Not so, however: her love for Jesus in the Blessed Sacrament was too great; her desire to see this mystery honoured by a special Feast too sincere, to allow her to be easily discouraged. Whatever opposition she met with, it only had the effect of making her pray with more fervour than before (if this were possible) for the success of the work. She never for one moment lost her calmness and tranquillity, but always tempered her zeal with discretion and prudence, so that while never allowing her ardour and zeal to slacken in the

least degree, she nevertheless kept it within just
and moderate bounds. But however much zeal
and ardour, however much prudence and discretion she might display, the bishop always kept to
his old answer: " We cannot rashly institute a
new Feast upon the mere vision of a woman."
Doubtless, Juliana had learned this answer of the
bishop, from those of her friends who had been
so zealous in soliciting him to institute the Feast
in his diocese. Whether she had or not, it
is certain that she never ceased to beg of God to
convince the bishop of His Will in the matter.
She represented to her Lord that He had urged
her to solicit this Feast; that she herself was
utterly incapable of bringing the thing to a successful termination, and she begged of Him, that
since the work was entirely His, and not hers,
to put forth His Almighty hand and finish His
work.

At length, when there seemed no probability
(humanly speaking) of the bishop ever giving up
his prejudices in this matter, God, Who had now
sufficiently tried the patience of His servant
Juliana, put forth His hand, and what could not
be accomplished by natural means, He Who can
do all things, accomplished by supernatural means.
Nothing less than a miracle was required to convert the bishop from his prejudices; nothing but
the power of God could determine him to listen
to those who were constantly soliciting him to
institute the Feast of Corpus Christi, and this
power God now exercised. Man could do nothing:
man had done all he could to convince the bishop
of the utility of the project, but without avail;
God Himself, therefore, undertakes to convince
the bishop, and reveals to him that it is His Will
that the Feast should be instituted, and that the
bishop must no longer oppose it.

How this revelation was made to the bishop we do not know; whether the Will of God was made known to him by an angel, or whether God spoke to him in prayer, is uncertain. But the bishop must have had the revelation in 1244, for, according to several historians, and among others the Bollandists, who in this respect are of great authority, the bishop had to wait two years after he received the revelation, before he could institute the Feast. Now, the Feast was instituted in his diocese in 1246, consequently he had this revelation in 1244.

Some authors say that the bishop was on a journey when God made known to him His Will; be this as it may, it is certain that the bishop lost no time in communicating to Juliana what had happened. He therefore seized the first opportunity that presented itself of visiting Cornillon and its holy prioress. As soon as he saw her, and the first salutations were over, the bishop told her that he had received from God a very singular grace and benefit, by which he had learned that it was the Will of God that a Feast should be instituted in honour of the most Holy Sacrament of the Altar; that, although he had hitherto refused to listen to the solicitations made to him for its institution, he could now do so no longer, because the hand of God had touched him, and he now knew it to be the Will of God that this Feast should be instituted, and that he dare no longer resist His Will.

Juliana was filled with joy and consolation upon listening to this discourse of the bishop; and as she recognised in this the finger of God, it was to Him that she poured out her heart in fervent thanksgivings for so great a benefit.

From this time the bishop's zeal for the institution of the Feast was most ardent; but many unforeseen events arose which obliged him to defer for a time its institution. During this time the bishop had recourse to Juliana, to beg her prayers for the removal of these obstacles; he himself used every effort to forward the work he now had so much at heart.

At length, an opportunity being afforded him, he assembled his synod, and proposed to them the institution of the Feast of Corpus Christi. The most venerable, religious and learned amongst them applauded the bishop's zeal, and begged him to institute the Feast; suggesting to him that it would be a very praiseworthy action for him to institute this Feast, and thus recognise and exalt this gift of Divine grace. " Viri venerabiles et religiosi solemnitatis ordinem et processum exposuerunt reverendo Patri domino Roberto Leodiensi episcopo et eidem ut divinæ munus gratiæ agnosceret et exaltaret, verbis efficacibus suggesserunt."

The bishop, full of his object, and full of zeal for its accomplishment, wished to follow at once the advice of his clergy. He therefore immediately published the following pastoral, which proves how much ardour and zeal he had for the institution of the solemnity.

" Robert, by the grace of God, Bishop of Liège, to our beloved children in Christ, the Abbots, Priors, Deans, Presbyters, and other ecclesiastics in the diocese of Liège, health and abundance of grace.

" Among the many wonderful and admirable works which the Lord our God, Who is wonderful in all His works, hath operated, there is one which, more than all others, on account of its great sublimity, merits all our admiration and gratitude : and this, is that ineffable Sacrament of

Christ's sacred Body and Blood, in which He hath
given Himself for food to them that fear Him,
and which He hath bequeathed to us as a wonderful and delectable memorial of His Passion. The
Royal Psalmist having entered into the abyss of
the Divine mysteries, hath congratulated us upon
them a long time before, singing in these words:
' He hath made a remembrance of His wonderful
works, being a merciful and gracious Lord; He
hath given food to them that fear Him.' If God,
Who hath for ever been mindful of His testament,
spoke of this mystery by the mouth of His prophet, and after having established it, hath again
commanded us to be mindful of it, saying: ' As
often as ye shall do this, ye shall do it for a commemoration of Me,' we ought not to be thought
worthy of blame, if, besides the daily commemoration which is made of this admirable Sacrament,
in the Sacrifice of the Mass; we resolve, in order
to confute the foolishness of heretics, and to assist
our feeble memories, that once a year this precious, venerable, and unspeakable Sacrament shall
be recalled to the memory of all the faithful, in a
more special and solemn manner than it is in the
daily Sacrifice of the Mass.

"Seeing that the saints, whom the Church
daily invokes and commemorates in the Litanies,
in the Mass, and in certain prayers, have, nevertheless, one special day in each year, on which
their virtues and singular merits are brought before us, we think it to be most worthy, just, and
salutary, that the most Holy Sacrament, the sweetness of all sweetnesses, should have upon earth a
special solemnity, in order to render most singular
and great thanks to our Lord God, because He
hath, out of His most pure, unspeakable and inestimable charity, given Himself to us in this
Sacrament, and daily wonderfully offers Himself

upon our altars. In this offering of Himself, He
ceases not, nor will He ever cease, to fulfil that
His most sweet promise, saying : ' Behold I am
with you always, even to the consummation of the
world.' It is, moreover, in this Sacrament that,
He is mindful of His other words : ' My delights
are to be with the children of men.' This solemnity of which we speak, would contribute much to
supply for the omissions and irreverences which
we commit in the celebration of the holy mysteries.

" Who is there among the faithful, therefore,
who can doubt that this solemnity will tend to the
honour and glory of God, the increase of faith,
hope, charity and all other virtues, and the great
benefit and profit of all the elect of God ?

" Desiring that these blessings may be bestowed
upon the flock committed to our care, and desiring
to excite human forgetfulness and negligence to
render the thanks that are due to the Lord for so
great a gift, we ordain, and we command it to be
inviolably observed by you, that every year, upon
the Thursday after Trinity Sunday, you celebrate
the Feast of the most Holy Sacrament, and that
you recite its Office of nine lessons, with proper
responsories, versicles and antiphons, a copy of
which we will send to you. This Feast shall be
perpetually and inviolably observed by you, and
we command that the people abstain from all
servile work, as on Sundays. Moreover, the
clergy shall, upon the Sunday preceding the Feast,
direct the people confided to their care, to fast
upon the vigil of the said Feast, and shall also
exhort them, in order that they may obtain the
remission of their sins, to prepare themselves for
it by prayers, watchings, alms-deeds and other
good works, that thus being well prepared they
may, upon the Feast, devoutly receive this most

sweet and holy Sacrament; but in this matter we wish to constrain no one. We hope that, upon the occasion of this Feast, God, and His Son Jesus Christ, will be pleased with the sacrifice of expiation we offer to Them, and that They will be moved to show mercy to the world, which is now, by so much wickedness, hurrying on to speedy ruin and shipwreck."

This pastoral of the bishop is dated 1246. He ordered twenty copies of the Office which had been composed by John, now Prior of Cornillon, to be distributed in different districts of his diocese. But the bishop, after having instituted the Feast, did not live to see its celebration. He was, soon after the publication of his pastoral, stricken with the sickness of which he died. Doubtless God was satisfied with the zeal he had manifested so far, and without requiring more of him, called him to receive the reward of his labours. When the bishop was first taken ill, he promised, that if God should restore him to health, he would devote himself, with more earnestness than before, to spread devotion to the Blessed Sacrament. As death approached, he exhorted all who assisted at it, with more fervour than ever, to do all they could, in order to celebrate the new Feast upon the appointed day, with all possible devotion and piety. He begged them to use every endeavour to enkindle in the hearts of the faithful a great devotion to the Sacrament of the Altar, assuring them that they could do nothing more pleasing and acceptable to the Lord.

But the bishop's piety was not content with merely exhorting his attendants to devotion to the Sacrament of Love; he wished to give in his own person an example of this devotion. He was unable to be carried to the church, on account of the grievous nature of his sickness; but, in order to satisfy his devotion to the Holy Eucharist, he caused the Office of the new Feast to be recited in his chamber, and joined in it with the greatest possible devotion and piety.

Thus died this good bishop, giving us in his own person an evident proof that Juliana's vision came from God. For who but God could so have changed the bishop's sentiments? At first he was not only indifferent to the institution of the new Feast, but even opposed, and strongly opposed to it. Every effort was used to change his opinion, but in vain ; then it was that God, in order to show that Juliana was led by the good Spirit, Himself changed the bishop's sentiments, which could not have been changed by any other power than His, Who ruleth, governeth, and disposeth all things, according to His good pleasure.

Eva, the recluse of St. Martin's, having heard of the death of the bishop, sent a messenger to announce it to Juliana; but God had already revealed it to her, for as soon as she saw Eva's messenger, she said, "You have not brought me good news, but bad ; the bishop is dead." The messenger was greatly astonished at this, for she knew Juliana could not know this by any human means, but she simply said to the Saint : "Yes, it is so, the bishop is dead ; and I have come to tell you the news."

Although the institution of the Feast of Corpus Christi had been proclaimed by episcopal authority, nevertheless there was little eagerness manifested for its celebration. Indeed, it almost seemed as if the bishop's pastoral had but made the people less desirous than ever for the celebration of the new Feast. The zeal and ardour of the bishop appeared to meet with nothing but coldness and neglect. The devil, who well knew that the cele-

bration of this Feast would tend to the greater
glory of God, did all in his power to prevent it.
He could not now prevent its institution, at least
in the Diocese of Liège, but he was resolved to do
all he could to prevent its celebration. This great
enemy of all that is good, therefore, moved some
to oppose it ; others to treat it with indifference ;
others to consider it as an innovation ; in fine, in
a thousand ways he raised up obstacles to the
celebration of the Feast.

Juliana, who placed all her hopes in God, when
she saw the celebration of the Feast surrounded
with so many difficulties, had recourse to Him,
Who always listens to His faithful servants. He
heard her, and although her desires were not as
yet fully satisfied, God did not, however, entirely
leave His servant without consolation. Our Saint
had always been in high favour with the canons of
the collegiate church of St. Martin, and she spoke
to them so movingly upon the celebration of the
Feast, that they resolved to comply with the decree
issued by the bishop. John of Lausanne, whom,
the reader will remember, had already been a friend
to our Saint upon many occasions, also strongly
supported her representations, so that the chapter
of St. Martin's unanimously resolved to celebrate
the Feast upon the very day appointed by the
bishop. The bishop had, by his pastoral, instituted the Feast in 1246 ; but the day he appointed
for its first celebration was the Thursday after
Trinity Sunday, in the year 1247 ; it was upon
this day that the canons of St. Martin first celebrated the Feast of Corpus Christi, with all possible splendour, magnificence and devotion.

It is easier to imagine than to describe the joy
of Juliana, Eva, Isabella of Huy, and the others,
who had been so zealous in promoting the institution of this Feast, when they saw their desires for

the first time satisfied by its celebration. But
although there were many reasons to rejoice and
be glad, yet, notwithstanding, Eva had many
doubts and fears, concerning the ultimate success
of the undertaking. In the whole diocese of
Liège, she saw only one church complying with
the orders of the bishop. There were even some
to be found who openly opposed the celebration of
the Feast, and declared it to be an innovation, or
at least a singularity. Seeing this, and knowing
that the universal Church had not yet spoken, she
had great fears for its success. Eva communicated
these fears to Juliana ; but the latter removed her
fears by a very consoling prediction. "Cease, my
dear Eva," she said to her, "cease to trouble
yourself; the decrees of God are infinitely of more
weight and value than those of men ; what He has
resolved upon, He will establish so firm and solid,
that all the efforts of men to overthrow His work
will be vain and useless. There will, I assure
you, come a time when the Feast will be celebrated, not only in the Diocese of Liège, but also
throughout the universal Church. All Christendom shall receive it; all the faithful will greatly
rejoice in its celebration ; it will be a Feast of joy
and triumph throughout the whole Church. It
is true many obstacles will have to be overcome ; there will be much opposition, but who
can fight against God ? or who can resist His
Will ?"

Happily we have seen the accomplishment of
this prediction of Juliana. In every part of the
Catholic world this Feast is now celebrated with
gladness and joy, with piety and devotion : all
that is beautiful in nature or art ; all that is
splendid, grand, and magnificent, Catholic piety
now uses to render this Feast more solemn and
imposing. It is everywhere considered as a Feast

of triumph. Jesus, it is true, has been blasphemed in the very sacrament in which He hath shown all the riches of His boundless love; but, to atone for these blasphemies, as far as possible, the faithful throughout the world, upon each recurrence of this Feast of Corpus Christi, seem to vie with each other in rendering homage, respect, veneration, and adoration, to the King of kings and the Lord of lords, who is truly present in this sacrament of love.

Thus we see that Juliana's prediction is accomplished to the very letter; and the foresight of all this honour and glory rendered to God by the celebration of this Feast, must have been a source of great and abundant consolation to our saint in all her troubles and trials. So that she could well say with St. Paul: "Blessed be the God and Father of our Lord Jesus Christ, the Father of mercies, and the God of all consolation, who consoleth us in all our tribulations."*

CHAPTER XII.

MORE TROUBLES AT CORNILLON.

JULIANA, as we have seen in the preceding chapters, having already experienced many contradictions and much persecution, had endured all with patience and resignation; thus she had prepared herself to receive one of the greatest graces God bestows upon His elect: more crosses. The lives of the saints always present to us these features; crosses, tribulations and afflictions. If

* 2 Cor. i.

they have their consolations, they have their corresponding trials; they have to suffer and endure the persecutions and assaults of the demons, to struggle against their own nature, and they are hated and despised by the world. Our Lord Himself declared that this last would be the portion of His true disciples. "If the world hate you," He says, "know ye that it hath hated Me before you. If you had been of the world, the world would love its own; but because you are not of the world, but I have chosen you out of the world, therefore the world hateth you."* Our Blessed Lord here gives us the secret of the world's utter incapability of enduring the saints, "because He has chosen them out of the world, therefore the world hateth them." No wonder that it should be so; the maxims and ways of the saints are entirely different to those of the world. The saints seek after God alone, but the world understands nothing of those mysterious and intimate relations and attractions which unite the soul to God. Those who follow the ordinary ways of life, generally prosper in the world; but the saints, whom God usually conducts by extraordinary ways, appear in the world as strangers and foreigners, as inhabitants of a superior world in the midst of society. The order of society is for the saints disorder, and they are for society an object of scandal; thus, no place is found for them in the world. Earth is not their centre of gravity, they cannot place their feet upon it. They are more accustomed to fly than walk; their centre of gravity is God, to Him they continually tend; by Him they are constantly attracted. Their souls are tuned after quite another scale than that of ordinary souls, and nothing but the greater honour and glory of God

---

* St. John, xv. 18, 19.

is to them harmonious. Nature and society are too strong and powerful to be turned from their ordinary, low, groveling ways by the exhortations and examples of the saints, however powerful these exhortations and examples may be; the saints have, therefore, to suffer all the consequences of the discord there is between themselves and the world. They have consequently to suffer physically, by sickness, infirmities, and pains of every kind; and they have to suffer morally, by continual trials, which assist them to overcome their nature completely, and which also give them an opportunity of practising patience and resignation in the most heroic degree.

Juliana was no exception to this general law: she, like other saints, suffered physically and morally. We have seen how patiently she bore her former trials, we have now to see her exposed to new ones. As soon as Bishop Robert, who had protected her, was dead, her enemies again sought to persecute her, and she soon became the victim of their malice. The episcopal see having been vacant a year; in the midst of many troubles and much discord, Henry of Gueldre at length obtained the dignity. He certainly was not a very fit subject for a bishop; he was more like a prince than a bishop, extremely devoted to pleasure, having more the spirit of a warrior than a shepherd and pastor of souls, and seeking for anything and everything but peace.

All the historians of Liège are unanimous in describing the period of Henry's administration as one of the most disastrous for the country, as well morally, as also for that which regards the material peace of the country. Some writers, however, out of enmity to the Church, have greatly exaggerated these evils, in order thus to bring discredit upon religion. Fortunately, these disorders will not

enter much into our narrative; we shall dwell on
them as little as possible, and only as much as
will be necessary to the elucidation of our history.
If the reader wishes to know the true history of
these times of disorder, he may consult the works
of Chapeauville, Fisen, and Foullon, who have
faithfully related, under its true point of view, the
unworthy conduct of Henry of Gueldre.

It was under the government of this prelate, so
little worthy of being one, that a storm once more
arose in Cornillon, and Juliana became its principal
victim.   Some of the brethren of the monastery
of Cornillon had never been well satisfied with
the election of John; these monks loved the
licence that the irregularities of Roger gave them,
far better than the strict monastic discipline that
John adhered to.   They therefore desired nothing
more ardently than the return of Roger.   It is
some consolation for us to know that these disaffected monks did not form the majority of the
community, but were only a minority, strong
enough, however, to cause much trouble, and
eventually entirely to overthrow all regularity and
discipline.

After the deposition of Roger and the return of
Juliana, which we have related in a previous
chapter, Bishop Robert made some wise regula-
tions for the good of both houses.   As long as
this bishop lived the bad monks were able to
accomplish nothing; but no sooner was he dead,
than they recalled Roger from the monastery of
Huy where he had been banished.   In order the
better to succeed in their design, they did not at
once receive him as prior, but only as one deprived
of all dignity.   To have replaced him in his former
dignity all at once, after his having been so publicly deposed, would have been too flagrant an
act of injustice.   They therefore went quietly to

work, and received him first as a simple monk.
Then they began to persecute the Prior John in
every way they could ; they began also to spread
various reports, insinuating that Roger had not
been fairly dealt with, that his crimes had been
exaggerated, &c. Then they began to speak
against John, and to say all manner of evil things
concerning him. At length their violence broke
out openly, and they chased John from the house
altogether. They did not, however, at once replace
Roger in his former dignity, but substituted in
John's place for the present a monk of another
Order.

Juliana, however, knew very well to what this
state of things would tend ; she knew they
aimed at nothing less than the restoration of
Roger, and that if they succeeded in their evil
designs, they would then be sure to persecute
both her and her sisters. For, so long as she
remained near at hand, they knew she would do
all in her power to procure the re-establishment
of proper order. It was quite evident to Juliana
that they could have no other motive for chasing
away John, than the desire of again making Roger
the prior. But, in the midst of all these troubles,
she continued to lead those committed to her care
in the paths of religious perfection, and preserved
in her own house the regularity and discipline,
which the monks were endeavouring to overthrow
in theirs.

John was a wise, prudent, faithful, holy religious, whom no one could with truth charge with
a single breach of his holy rule. Juliana, who
respected his many virtuous qualities, was eager
to console him in his tribulations. She represented to him the examples of the saints, who
have all been purified in the furnace of affliction,
and have always manifested great courage in

adversities; that their courage should animate
him to constancy in good, and their example
move him to exercise charity towards his enemies.

Our saint knew full well that in a very short
time the storm would reach both her and her
sisters; for this reason she now exhorted them
with more fervour than ever (if this were possible)
to the practice of good works. She prepared them
little by little for the persecutions she knew were
not far distant. In her exhortations she frequently dwelt upon the advantages to be derived
from adversities and tribulations; she reminded
them that in this manner virtue is tried and per-
fected; that a life exempt from trials is not the
portion of God's elect; that the kingdom of heaven
suffereth violence, and that the violent bear it
away; that, in fine, as spouses of Jesus
Christ they should be willing and ready to endure
all kinds of sufferings and pains, yea, even persecutions and exile. These exhortations of the holy
mother confirmed her daughters in the resolution
of adhering faithfully to their rule and to their
lawful prioress, and also prepared them to resist
the coming storm, the dark clouds of which were
already visible in the horizon.

The designs of the partizans of the deposed
Prior Roger were at length openly and clearly
manifested, for they re-established him in his
former dignity. Whether the disaffected monks
had intimidated the rest, or had unfortunately
drawn them over to their own way of thinking, or
had restored Roger in spite of them, we do not
know; whichever way it was, Roger was again
prior.

Juliana, however, constantly and firmly refused
to acknowledge any other prior than John; whatever bad treatment she had to suffer from Roger's

partizans, she would never acknowledge him as prior. Roger and his friends then clearly saw that so long as Juliana was in the way, their designs could never be accomplished, for they well knew that Juliana would, as soon as possible, take steps to remove this scandal and render justice to John. They therefore determined to get rid of Juliana cost what it might.

Roger's friends knew that this would be no easy task; how were they to succeed in driving away one whose reputation for virtue and sanctity was so great? They were not ignorant that her holy manner of living had acquired for her great credit with the principal ecclesiastics and dignitaries of the Church of Liège. They knew that it was on her account that Roger had formerly been deposed, and that so long as she remained Prioress of Cornillon, Roger could not peacefully enjoy the dignity to which he had just been restored. This thought animated the adherents of Roger to use every exertion to force Juliana once more into exile.

This, however, they found to be no easy task, justice was most certainly and evidently on Juliana's side; but what they could not hope to obtain by means of justice, they endeavoured to obtain by violence. Juliana's zeal for the institution of the Feast of Corpus Christi was again made use of to render her unpopular. Her enemies represented her as a turbulent woman, who, under the pretext of piety and devotion, sought to bring in innovations and overthrow all public order. But they were not content with this; they accused her of endeavouring to set aside her rule and constitutions, and further declared her to be a hypocrite, proud, rebellious, factious, in fine, everything that was bad. These calumnies having been well circulated, Juliana soon became again the object of derision and persecution. They endeavoured by every means to take away from her all peace and tranquillity; they tried to intimidate her by threats, and they heaped upon her all kinds of injuries in order to force her once more to abandon her home. But it was Juliana's duty to remain at her post, as long as there remained the slightest hope of justice being obtained. There was also a still more cogent reason for remaining, and that was the necessity she was under of leading the souls confided to her care in the paths of Christian perfection, and keeping them to the strict observance of their holy Rule and Constitutions. She was not ignorant of the words of our Lord: "The good shepherd giveth his life for the sheep. But the hireling and he that is not the shepherd, whose own the sheep are not, seeth the wolf coming, and leaveth the sheep, and flieth: and the wolf snatcheth and scattereth the sheep. The hireling flieth because he is a hireling, and hath no care for the sheep."* Our good shepherdess, therefore, in spite of all persecutions, remained to take care of the sheep. The wolves might howl and assail her as much as they pleased, but so long as they did not harm her sheep, she cared not, she remained firm as a rock in the midst of the tempest. The time was to come when she would have to sacrifice herself for the sake of her flock; but so long as the least hope remained of preserving her sheep from the ravening wolves, she kept firm and constant to her post.

The malice of Juliana's enemies was not yet satisfied, their aim was to excite the populace against her: the mob always being ready for acts of violence, and usually acting without reason,

---

* S. John, x., 11, 12, 13.

above all, if they can be persuaded that their
rights and privileges have been infringed. Unhappily, the adherents of Roger lived in times which
were very propitious for the success of their factious
designs. The city of Liège at this period offered
a terrible spectacle of strife, troubles, dissensions,
and animosities.

Henry of Gueldre, although certainly very unfit
to be a bishop, had nevertheless been legitimately
elected to the dignity; but some who had desired
the bishopric endeavoured to prove that his election was not valid, and they and their party created
disturbances in the city, which ended at last in
open riot and sedition. The streets and public
places were filled with tumultuous assemblages,
nothing was heard and seen but threats, combats,
and projects of sedition; in fine, men's minds
were filled with thoughts of strife, revenge, and
anything and everything but peace.

Roger and his friends took advantage of this
disturbed state of society to raise up a bitter persecution against Juliana. They joined themselves
to the dregs of the excited people, spoke so much
evil against our saint, and so forcibly persuaded
the mob that she was an enemy to their rights
and privileges, and that she wanted to force upon
them the celebration of a Feast that was a
singularity and an innovation; in fine, they spread
amongst the people so many calumnious reports
of the holy mother; that the mob were enraged
against her, to such a degree, as to be ready for
any deeds of malice and violence.

The mob, thus excited, ran with shouts, vocife-
rations, and imprecations to the oratory of Juliana,
thinking to find her there; they took up stones
and cudgels, (the usual arms of an excited mob,)
and broke all the windows of our saint's retreat.
But this, of course, was not sufficient to satisfy

their malice and revenge; they therefore armed
themselves with pikes, hammers, and hatchets,
burst open the doors, broke in the roofs, and threw
down the walls.   This storm burst forth so suddenly, that they had scarcely time to save Juliana
from its violence; she, however, would not abandon her daughters until they had been secured,
as well as might be, from danger.   The maddened
populace, in the hope of finding Juliana in the
common dormitory, ascended thither, and speedily
commenced the work of its destruction.   One of
the first who laid his sacrilegious hands upon the
edifice, was struck with a most painful wound,
which he bore unto the day of his death, although
every remedy was employed to heal it.

Juliana, in the midst of this dreadful tempest,
never uttered the least word of impatience or
anger, but remained calm, tranquil, and peaceful
in the midst of it all.   She did not for a moment
lose the recollection of God's presence; but even
when the noise and hubbub was at its greatest
height, she was closely and intimately united to
God, adoring His Holy Will, which had permitted
these things to happen, and, after the example of
her Saviour, she prayed most fervently for her
enemies, and she also exhorted her daughters to do
the same.

The enemies of Juliana did all they could to
induce her to acknowledge Roger as prior, but
could never succeed.   If she would have done so,
her enemies would have left her in peace and
tranquillity; but neither the pretexts which men
interested in these matters alleged to her, nor
threats, nor injuries, nor bad treatment, could
induce her to recognise any one but John for
prior.   She had too keen a sense of justice to do
otherwise; he had been truly, validly, and legitimately elected prior; he was worthy of the office;

him, and him alone, therefore, would she acknowledge as prior.

Roger's friends and partizans, however, were determined to drive Juliana from her home, and they never relaxed in their efforts to attain this end. Juliana was now convinced that if she did not wish some harm to happen to her daughters, she must depart. She saw plainly that unless she did so, her enemies would completely destroy the house, and would not leave one stone upon another. In this case, some injury would be sure to be done to her daughters, and therefore she resolved to sacrifice herself for the sake of her children, and in order to avoid the commission of new crimes. When the holy mother communicated this intention of hers to her daughters, they all wished to accompany her, promising to share with her all the poverty and inconveniences of exile; they were so devoted to their good mother, and so persuaded of the justice of her cause, that they would have endured anything, rather than be separated from her. Juliana, however, did not as yet know where to find an asylum for herself, and therefore could not be charged with such a numerous train. She chose only three, viz., Isabella, Agnes, and Ozila, upon whose constancy and fidelity she could depend. She exhorted all to endure patiently the sufferings and trials it might please the Lord to send them, reminding them how much Jesus hath suffered for us, and with what patience and love He bore all that the malice of His enemies could invent to torment Him. She implored those she did not take with her to remain tranquilly in the convent, and keep faithfully to the strict observance of their rule.

The time for parting at length arrived, and, amid the tears and lamentations of all, she tore herself from the arms of her daughters, and went to seek out of the house the peace she could not find in it. Her children, who loved her so dearly, were never again to see her face in this world. Never again, was she to enter the doors of that holy house in which she had received so many divine consolations. She had no certain place of refuge; as yet she knew not the home the Lord had prepared for her: she went forth trusting entirely in the goodness and bounty of God. As the sisters noticed that Juliana took nothing with her, they asked her what resources she had to procure her livelihood. "None but Providence," she replied, "and if we come to be in want of the necessities of life, two of us will beg from door to door to procure them for us."

It may doubtless seem to some a strange thing that a man of such dissolute manners, and of such bad reputation as Roger was, could succeed in driving from her house a superioress who was so very holy; but, unhappily, the city of Liège at this period was full of disorders, tumults, and discord. The bishop was more like a prince than a pastor of souls; he was more occupied with military and family affairs than with the care of his bishoprick. The whole city offered to the contemplation of beholders a picture of anarchy, confusion, and discord; the perpetrators of crimes of every kind walked with head erect, and remained unpunished. The roads were full of robbers, and good people dared not complain, for fear of experiencing still greater evils. In the midst of such general confusion and disorder, Juliana was without a single friend or protector, who dared to defend her cause, or even to give her an asylum, because Roger had procured for his friends and partizans all the most dissolute and daring men who then, unfortunately, enjoyed the greatest credit. Roger had chosen his time well, and made good use of it; Juliana's zeal for the institution of the new Feast had furnished him with one means of exciting the mob against her; many other calumnies were invented and circulated against her, and so this unworthy prior and his friends succeeded in stirring up the populace to drive away our saint. Too much disorder and tumult then existed in the place for justice to be done; thus it was that wickedness and crime triumphed, but innocence and virtue were left undefended.

Juliana, in the midst of these mortifications and disasters, far from allowing the least murmur to escape her lips, was, on the contrary, willing to lay down her life, if, by so doing, she could have rendered any service to her enemies. When some of her friends asked her how she could pray so fervently for men who were so enraged against her, and so determined to ruin her, the holy mother answered: "Because I desire their salvation as much as my own." Thus did this faithful spouse of Jesus Christ most faithfully imitate Him in His charity towards His enemies, and like Him, the only words she uttered concerning her bitterest persecutors, was a prayer that God would pardon them: "Father, forgive them, for they know not what they do."

CHAPTER XIII.

FURTHER PROGRESS OF THE INSTITUTION OF THE FEAST.

It was in the year 1248, that Juliana was driven this second time from her convent. The dissension and discord then prevalent lasted for several years; the different factions became more and more enraged against each other, so that the hope of returning peace became day by day more feeble. Almighty God, having waited long and patiently for this rebellious people to return to good, at length stretched forth His hand to chastise them. In 1252 there arose in the unfortunate city of Liège, a sedition which was the source of an infinity of evils, not only to the city itself, but also to the whole diocese. Hocsemius, and other writers, have left us [a description of these evils and miseries, which is as faithful as it is terrible. "The avenging hand of God," says Hocsemius, "weighed so heavily upon the whole country, that I believe none escaped its blows. In the city and diocese of Liège, people of every condition, ecclesiastical or secular, priests and laymen, rich and poor, high and low, great and small, men and women, all were exposed to the tempest. Everywhere, houses were destroyed; the rich were despoiled of their goods; those of moderate fortune impoverished and reduced to mendicity. Nothing was heard of but robberies, brigandage, combats, assassinations, violence; in fine, every kind of evils, scandals and calamities. By which we may be persuaded that God punishes the wicked for their crimes, although He does not always deliver the just from their tribulations; because sufferings are always serviceable to God's elect." In order to ameliorate this sad state of things, they created two burgomasters, whose office it was to put down every riot and sedition upon its very first appearance, and before it had reached such dimensions as to render the task extremely difficult, and even, in some cases, almost impossible. It was their duty to suppress immediately everything that could tend to disturb the peace of the citizens.

Juliana having departed from Cornillon without the least hope of her returning, there was some foundation for fearing that the institution of the Feast of Corpus Christi, which she had so much at heart, would fall into oblivion. But it was not merely Juliana's work, it was the work of God, and therefore could not remain imperfect.

The reader will remember that Hugh of St. Cher, the Provincial of the Dominicans, had been one of the most ardent promoters of the institution of the Feast of Corpus Christi, as soon as he knew the vision Juliana had received concerning this matter. He was now a Cardinal, and was much esteemed for his erudition, piety and learning. He has written some learned commentaries on the Holy Scriptures, and a concordance of the Bible, which is much valued. He had assisted at the Council of Lyon, in 1245, and it was then that he was created Cardinal, under the title of St. Sabina. He had been employed by the Pope upon several occasions, in which great skill and prudence were required, and had always acquitted himself of the duties confided to him, in a manner which gave entire satisfaction to all parties concerned.

He was now a legate of the Holy See, and had been sent to Liège to remedy the irregularities, and put an end to the scandals then prevalent in the city and diocese. Those who were the most ardent supporters of the establishment of the Feast of Corpus Christi, spoke to the Cardinal of the decree of the late Bishop Robert, touching its institution. They also told him that the canons of St. Martin had faithfully and zealously celebrated the Feast, as the bishop had ordained. The Cardinal requested to see the Office which John, the late Prior of Cornillon, had composed, and after examining it, he approved it, and entirely confirmed it ; moreover, he wished to celebrate the Feast himself, and sing the Mass. He appointed a day for this purpose, and a great concourse of people assisted at it. The Cardinal, clothed with his pontifical robes, ascended the pulpit, and delivered a most eloquent discourse upon the necessity of this solemnity, and upon the treasures of grace the people would receive from its celebration.

This approbation, coming from such a man as the Cardinal of St. Sabina, had great weight, and went very far towards dissipating the prejudices of many who had hitherto opposed the celebration of the Feast. The great prelate, upon this occasion, preached with so much unction, so pathetically and so eloquently, that a canon of Liège, whose name was Stephen, was greatly moved by it. Being struck with the sublimity of the mystery, which had been the subject of the sermon, he told his sister that the Cardinal had persuaded him by his eloquence, and that he now firmly believed that this Feast was instituted for the greater honour and glory of God. He further declared that if he was permitted to alter his will, he would gladly bequeath an annuity, in order that the Feast might henceforth be celebrated with greater magnificence. His sister, who had been declared the sole heiress of his possessions, and whose devotion to the Blessed Sacrament was quite as great as her brother's, persuaded him to do as he desired, and so he altered his will. By mutual consent, they bequeathed to the Church of St. Martin an ample revenue, by which the canons were henceforth enabled to celebrate the Feast with greater splendour than heretofore.

The sister of this canon, no doubt, was extremely willing to consent to this bequest, both on account of her great devotion to the Blessed Sacrament, and also by reason of the friendship she had contracted with Juliana ; for she well knew how ardently our Saint desired that this Feast should be celebrated with all possible devotion, splendour and magnificence. Juliana had, by her prayers, upon one occasion, obtained a great favour for this lady. Her brother Stephen had, some years before, been desirous of abandoning his canonry, in order to devote himself to parochial duties, in a parish near his native place. His sister, however, endeavoured to turn him from his purpose ; she did not like to lose her brother, and she was, moreover, persuaded that he would be of more service to the Church of God, by remaining where he was. But this lady's representations had little effect upon her brother, and he resolved to give up the canonry he held at Liège. The lady then addressed herself to Juliana, in order to derive some consolation from conversing with her. Juliana, after having prayed to the Lord, said to her : " Place all your confidence in God, and be assured He will return your brother to you ; for it is not His Will that your brother should resign the dignity he now enjoys."

Juliana's words were verified ; Stephen went to Châlons, his native place, in order to endeavour to obtain the care of a parish ; but having presented

11

himself to the bishop for examination, they simply
gave him a book to read, and although he was a
learned man, and a very able jurisconsult, yet he
could not read a single word. The canon, in utter
astonishment at so extraordinary and so sudden a
loss of memory, endeavoured to collect his vanished faculties, but in vain ; from which he concluded that God did not approve the change. He
therefore returned to Liège, and never afterwards
experienced the least difficulty in recalling to his
memory the things he had previously learned.

Almighty God bestowed several graces upon
both the canon and his sister, in recompense for
the zeal they had shown in supporting, as far as
they were able, the celebration of the new Feast.
Stephen's sister, not being able to walk, thought
if she could only be carried to the church, in
order that she might adore her Lord, and also
communicate, that our Lord would restore to her
the use of her limbs. It was done as she desired ;
she was carried to the church, she communicated,
and upon her return found herself entirely cured.
The rumour of what had happened was soon
spread through the city, and many of the faithful
were by it animated with zeal for the celebration
of the Feast of Corpus Christi.

The Cardinal of St. Sabina was not content
with having himself celebrated the new Feast ;
but he also did all he could to promote its celebration throughout the whole district of his legation.
For this purpose, he issued a pastoral to confirm
the decree of the deceased Bishop Robert, which
is as follows :

" Brother Hugh, by the Divine mercy, of the
title of St. Sabina, Cardinal Priest, and Legate of
the Apostolic See, to our beloved Brethren and
Children in Christ, the Archbishops and Bishops,

the Rectors, Deans, Archdeacons and all Ecclesiastics, and to all the Faithful within the limits of our Legation, health in the Lord.

"When we weigh, in the same balance, the merits of the human race, and the benefits conferred upon us by the Eternal Creator; when we compare one with the other, and reflect that the benefits exceed our merits as much and more than the ocean in immensity surpasses one drop of dew, we are smitten with great fear and trembling. Nor is it without a cause, since the judgment of right reason tells us, that if man is consumed in the service of God, as wax melteth away before the fire, nevertheless he cannot render to God the homage due to His Supreme Majesty. God, having created man from the dust of the earth, hath made him a fellow citizen of the angels; then, seeing that man, after having fallen, was groaning under the weight of sin, and was under the power of the evil one, God became man, and uniting human flesh to the Divinity in the ineffable mystery of the Incarnation, He poured forth His most Precious Blood to redeem us from the bondage under which we groaned.

"But this was not sufficient to satisfy His love for mankind. When about to suffer death for man, and after death to ascend triumphantly into heaven, He wished to give us more evident proofs of His love, and hath, therefore, left us His most sacred Body and Blood, hidden under the Sacramental species as under a most pure veil. He hath bequeathed to us this precious treasure, in order that, by its virtue and efficacy, we may be protected and delivered from the powers of darkness; and that by its operation our venial sins might be forgiven us, that we might receive strength to resist all temptations to mortal sin, and obtain grace to advance in the paths of perfec-

tion and virtue.   It was also our Lord's Will,
that in the participation of this Holy Sacrament,
we should have a continual remembrance of His
Passion, and that we should offer to Him, for so
great a benefit, a continual sacrifice of praise ;
since every moment He bestows innumerable
benefits upon us, and will continue to do so, until
we come to a perfect age, and to the possession of
the plenitude of His glory, where we shall be fed
with the Bread of Life, and shall drink at the
Fountain of Living waters.   These good things
are, however, offered to us who travel in this dark
vale of tears, and who are under the shadow of
death ; they are offered to us, I say, in the Blessed
Sacrament of the Eucharist, and faith discovers
the Lord hidden under the Sacramental veils.

"Although this venerable sacrament is daily
recalled to the memory of the faithful in the
Sacrifice of the Mass, nevertheless it is very just
that once a year a more special and solemn commemoration should be made of this august mystery, than that which is made daily, or than that
which is made on Holy Thursday.   For upon
this day holy mother Church is occupied in recalling to the minds of the faithful the mysteries of
our Lord's Passion, and thus this holy sacrament
is not, like the other mysteries of our holy
religion, solemnly commemorated.   We think it
cannot be deemed incongruous, if this Love of
loves, this Sweetness of all sweetnesses, should
have a special Feast, in which our daily negligences
and irreverences should be supplied and atoned
for, by a solemn act of adoration and reparation.

" Therefore we resolve, that upon the Thursday after the Octave of Pentecost, the Feast of
this most excellent Sacrament shall be observed
within all the limits of our legation.   We beg and
exhort you all, by virtue of the authority we

exercise, to celebrate this Feast upon the day appointed, in all public churches; and we desire you to recite the Office specially appointed for this Feast. Moreover, in all public churches, notice of the Feast shall be given to the faithful upon the preceding Sunday; and they shall be exhorted so to prepare for the celebration of this Feast, by vigils, prayers, alms-deeds, and other good works, that they may be able devoutly to receive this Holy Sacrament, and through its operation may obtain the fulfilment of their holy and just desires, and may be purged from all affection to sin. However, we wish not to bind any to the receiving of this Sacrament, but leave each to do so, or not, according as the Spirit of God shall touch their hearts.

"In order to animate the faithful to observe and celebrate this Feast with all possible devotion; to all those who, being truly penitent, shall have confessed their sins, and shall visit a church in which the Office of the Feast is celebrated, either on the day of the Feast, or on any day during the Octave, we grant one hundred days indulgence.

"Given at Liège, on the 29th of December, in the year of our Lord, 1253."

This Pastoral of the Cardinal of St. Sabina, was quite sufficient to induce all true children of the Church to celebrate the Feast devoutly. But, unhappily, there are many who, although they bear the name of children of the Church, are not so in reality, and who, sometimes through negligence, sometimes through obstinacy, do not comply with their mother's commands. While then the good rejoiced at the honour and glory that would be given to God by the celebration of this Feast; the indifferent and the bad, either took no notice of the matter, or murmured against it.

But the Cardinal of St. Sabina was not the only Legate of the Holy See who approved the Institution of the Feast. A year afterwards, Peter Capoche, a Cardinal and Apostolic Legate, was sent to Liège to appease some differences that had arisen between the bishop and clergy. He was many times spoken to by the supporters of the new Feast, who begged him to do all he could to further the good cause. They told him it had been instituted by the late Bishop Robert, and that its institution had been confirmed by an Apostolic Legate. Cardinal Capoche therefore examined the causes which had led to the institution of the Feast, and also the Office which had been composed by John, the late Prior of Cornillon. After a careful and scrupulous examination of the whole affair, he declared that God Himself had inspired the institution of this Feast, and that to oppose its celebration would be to oppose the Will of God. He approved and highly praised the decrees published by the late bishop and by the Cardinal of St. Sabina, and, following the example of the latter, he addressed himself to all the ecclesiastics of his legation. In order not to weary the reader by too frequent repetitions of the same thing, we merely give the substance of the pastoral of Cardinal Capoche, which is as follows:

" When the faithful apply themselves to the meditation of the excellencies of the Deity, their love to God and His Son Jesus Christ is augmented; their zeal is inflamed to honour Him with a worship proportioned to His infinite greatness, above all, when they call to mind, that man, having fallen from a state of innocence, through the craft of the devil, was redeemed by the outpouring of the Precious Blood of the Redeemer; and that this loving Lord and Saviour hath, the night before His Passion, instituted the Sacrament of the

Eucharist, in which He hath given us His most
sacred Body and Blood to be our food." He then
goes on to remind them that "The Cardinal of
St. Sabina, Legate of the Holy See in Lower-
Germany, had decreed that the ineffable Sacrament
of the Body and Blood of Jesus Christ should
each year be honoured by a special Festival." He
then declares that he, as successor to the Cardinal
of St. Sabina, in the office of Legate to the Holy
See, regarded this decree relative to the establishment of the new Feast, as very holy and praiseworthy; that he confirmed it by virtue of his
authority as Apostolic Legate, and forbade it to
be contradicted, under pain of incurring the indignation of God, and of His blessed Apostles Peter
and Paul. This Pastoral of Cardinal Capoche is
dated the 27th of December, 1254.

The decrees of both Cardinals, as well as that
of Bishop Robert, were preserved in the archives
of the collegiate church of St. Martin-au-Mont,
Liège. Thus was the institution of the Feast
of Corpus Christi approved by two Apostolic
Legates. But, unfortunately, the decrees were
observed only as long as the cardinals remained
in their legation. No sooner had they departed,
than their commands were no longer respected,
and no more attention was paid to them; above
all, in certain churches, where it had been judged
that the Feast was a novelty, and that they ought
to give no heed to it. Some of the principal
ecclesiastics, who had been of this opinion, were
highly indignant at these decrees of the Legates,
and after their departure published a contradictory
decree, by which they forbade the celebration of
the Feast. But God did not fail to punish this
audacity; a trustworthy historian assures us that
" God chastised the authors of this contradictory
decree, and their chastisement was so sudden and

so extraordinary, that people could plainly see the
cause that had drawn upon them this chastisement."

After the prohibition of these ecclesiastics, the
celebration of the solemnity was interrupted, except in the collegiate church of St. Martin,
where it was constantly celebrated. The work of
God always suffers contradictions; St. Teresa
assures us, that whenever she met with great
opposition in any of her foundations, she always
rejoiced, because she knew by it that the new
foundation would give great honour and glory to
God. For if the devil did not fear this, he would
never trouble himself to oppose the work. So it
was in this institution of the Feast of Corpus
Christi; the devil was jealous of the honour and
glory that would be given to God by its celebration, and he feared that it would be a means of
bringing back to God many souls, whom otherwise
he would have had in his power. Therefore he
did all he could to oppose the work, and seduced
many and powerful enemies to speak against it,
and do all they could to destroy it. But although
the malice of the evil one is great, the power of
God is infinitely greater; and, notwithstanding the
many obstacles and oppositions that the institution of the Feast of Corpus Christi met with, it
has been approved by Sovereign Pontiffs, and by a
General Council, and is now received and celebrated
by the whole Church with great joy and gladness.
It was at first assailed by many storms and tempests; but He who can say to the waves,
"Hitherto shalt thou come, and no further," ap-
peased also in His own good time this tempest.
"He rebuked the winds and the waves, and there
was a great calm."

CHAPTER XIV.

ST. JULIANA IN EXILE.

IT is now time to see what became of Juliana after having departed from Cornillon. She departed, as we have said, trusting entirely in the good Providence of God, and having no other resource than a lively faith and confidence in the goodness and bounty of Him "Who giveth meat to all in due season." The first place that Juliana applied to for shelter from the storm, was the Abbey of Robertmont, which was built by Godfrey of Steenes, in 1215, and enlarged by Lambert de la Pierre, who gave it to the Cistercian Order in 1225. The abbess of this house received Juliana with much charity and kindness, doing all she could to alleviate the pain that their exile might cause these devoted daughters to experience. But this abbey being situated in the neighbourhood of Cornillon, Juliana was too near her enemies to remain long in peace and tranquillity; they used every means in their power to compel her to leave her new home, and in the end succeeded, for Juliana, rather than be a means of disturbing the peace of the community, departed.

Juliana's next place of refuge was the Abbey of Val-Notre-Dame, near Huy, which was also a Cistercian house, and where she was received with all possible kindness and charity. Everything that the abbess and her daughters could do, to assist, comfort, and succour their persecuted sisters, was done. They were extremely grieved to see Juliana and her sisters reduced to such necessity, and consequently did everything that their charitable zeal could suggest, to make them forget the persecutions they had endured. But Juliana and her sisters were still too near their enemies to live in peace; it seems they were determined to have her far away from them, and that they dreaded nothing so much as her return to Cornillon. Juliana, who loved peace, and constantly sought after it, now believed that the only means of procuring it was to pass into a foreign land. She therefore consulted with her three companions, Isabella, Agnes, and Ozila, who all agreed to the proposition of Juliana. The city of Namur appearing to offer them a secure shelter from the storm, and a place of refuge from the violence and persecutions of their enemies; they resolved to go there, trusting that God would provide for them as He had done hitherto.

They, therefore, executed this design; but being in a strange country, and entirely unknown, they found no one willing to receive them. They were looked upon with suspicion, and regarded as wandering religious, whom it was a duty to avoid, rather than to receive. They had, therefore, to endure all the hardships, inconveniences and humiliations of the greatest poverty and indigence. Nevertheless, they suffered their misfortunes with heroic resignation and courage, and mutually exhorted each other to suffer with patience for the love of Him, who has suffered so much for the love of us. Not very long after their arrival at Namur, however, some religious gave them a shelter; but as these religious were themselves poor, they could do little beyond this, so that they still had to experience great poverty and distress.

At length God sent them a friend in the person of Himana of Hochestede, sister of Conrad, Arch-

bishop of Cologne. Our Saint became acquainted
with this charitable woman, who was Abbess of
Salsines, a Cistercian house, situated on the Sambre, near to Namur. It was founded by Godfrey,
Count of Namur, and Ermenson of Luxembourg,
his wife. At the request of the Count and Countess, Pope Innocent II. consecrated the church in
1130. The Count and Countess had themselves
laid the foundation of this house, and upon its
completion St. Bernard came in person to visit
and approve it.

Himana, the Abbess of this house, having heard
that the Prioress of Cornillon and her companions
were begging their bread, wrote to the Archdeacon
of Liège, in order to acquaint herself with the circumstances which had reduced them to so great
penury. The Archdeacon, whose name was John,
was a very charitable and pious man ; he knew all
the particulars of Juliana's case, and faithfully
communicated them to Himana, the Abbess of
Salsines. The Abbess, learning from this the
persecutions Juliana had suffered, and that she
was now without any fixed abode, was eager to
offer Juliana and her sisters a house which belonged to her, and which was situated near the
Church of St. Aubin. The Prioress of Cornillon
most gratefully and gladly accepted this generous
offer.

Juliana and her sisters remained some years in
this house, living very poorly; but tasting some of
those ineffable pleasures God frequently bestows
upon His chosen servants. At this time there
were two precious relics in the Church of St.
Aubin ; one of the true wood of the Cross, and the
other of the Precious Blood of our Lord and
Saviour. In being able to adore these sacred
relics, Juliana and her sisters believed themselves

amply recompensed for all the trials and tribulations they had undergone.

John, the Archdeacon of Liège, compassionating
the misfortunes of Juliana and her sisters, in order
to procure them a proper and commodious dwelling, purchased for them some land near the Church
of St. Symphorian ; upon which some cells might
be built, which Juliana, by the help and assistance
of some pious persons, caused to be constructed.
This establishment was very advantageous to them,
compared with the one they had hitherto occupied;
but, having no revenue, they still remained in
much poverty, and were often reduced to great
extremities.   Himana, the Abbess of Salsines,
being deeply grieved to see these religious, who
had given all their earthly goods to their convent,
in such distress and misery, interested herself to
procure these persecuted women some alleviation
in their distress, and at length obtained for them
an annual pension.   In order not to give an occasion for the criticisms and suspicions of those who
are ever ready to find fault, and carp against religious ;   and also, in order that they might not be
charged with a spirit of independence ;   Juliana
and her sisters submitted themselves to their bene-
factress, the Abbess of Salsines, and promised
obedience to her.

Juliana, through all the trials and misfortunes
that she had experienced, always remained the
same.   No murmurs, no complaints; she was
always meek, gentle, patient, resigned.   Her love
of prayer, her zeal for Evangelical perfection, never
relaxed.   She persevered in all her religious exercises, and in the practice of all good works.   Her
fervour never diminished, but always increased ;
and she practised the virtue of self-abnegation in
the most heroic degree.   God was her All, and

she could find Him in exile, as well as she could in her much-loved home at Cornillon.

Notwithstanding her great courage, and in spite of her firmness in patiently suffering all kinds of trials and persecutions, her health at last gave way. She had forced herself to endure pains and sufferings, but nature, at length, could endure no more. She became more feeble every day, and her sisters feared that the end had come. Juliana's companions were deeply afflicted at this; they thought their good mother was about to be taken from them, and that they should be left alone in a strange land, with few to care for, or think of them. So long as their dear mother was spared to them, they felt they could endure anything; but if she was taken from them, they thought that all their joy, comfort and consolation would depart with her. Juliana noticed their affliction, and as God had revealed to her that she would survive all her companions, she consoled them, and said: "My dear sisters, fear not, I shall be your faithful companion until death, for I shall survive you."

The sisters thought, at first, that these words of Juliana were merely uttered to console them; but they soon afterwards experienced the truth of her prediction. Agnes and Ozila died at Namur, and were interred at Salsines. The year of their death is not certainly known, some writers place it at 1254; in this case they had suffered with their holy prioress six years of exile; since, as we have said above, it was in the year 1248 that Juliana and her companions were driven from Cornillon. Agnes is mentioned in the Cistercian Menologium, on the twenty-first of January, and the title of Blessed is there given to her in these words: "At Namur died the blessed Agnes, sister of St. Juliana of Cornillon, who having attained a

high degree of sanctity, after many and great
labours, hath obtained eternal rest."* Ozila is
also mentioned in the same book, on the third of
January: "The blessed Ozila, virgin, companion
of St. Juliana of Cornillon, who embraced the
Cistercian institute in the Convent of Mount Cornillon, after many labours patiently endured, died
in exile at Namur, and was honourably buried at
Salsines." Raissius also, in his Belgica Chris-
tiana, gives them the title of Blessed.

Isabella of Huy was deeply afflicted at the loss
of her sisters, who had been so long her companions in exile. Knowing the sincere affection
that the Abbess of Salsines entertained for Juliana, she persuaded the latter to take up her abode
in the Abbey. She represented to our Saint, that
now there were only two left, a life in community
would be much more suitable to their condition;
that they were both advanced in age, that their
habitual infirmities had made them very weak and
delicate, so that they now required some care and
attention, and that this would sure to be bestowed
upon them at Salsines.

Juliana, however, foresaw the storms and tempests with which this abbey was threatened, and
was therefore, at first, reluctant to accede to the
wishes of Isabella; but the latter pressed our Saint
so much in this matter, that at length she consented. The Abbess Himana received them as
angels from heaven, hoping to profit much by
their holy conversation. She placed them in a
special and spacious apartment, and treated them
with the greatest consideration and respect. Juliana, who was an ardent lover of poverty, did not
altogether relish this splendour, and therefore
begged the abbess to place them in poorer apart-

* Cist. Men. 21 Jan.

ments. There was a very small cell near the church, which Juliana declared to the Abbess would be amply sufficient to satisfy her. Himana, however, thought she could never show too much respect to such deserving women; she, therefore, begged them to remain in the apartments which had been provided for them. Juliana, who knew that obedience is better than sacrifice, did as the abbess desired, and remained in her spacious apartments.

Juliana's stay at Salsines was of great utility to all the religious, who were greatly edified by the many virtues and angelic conversation, which it was impossible for our Saint altogether to hide. The Abbess Himana frequently entertained herself with Juliana, and the more she conversed with her, the more she discovered the singular virtues of our Saint. One day that they were conversing together, upon the canticle that the Blessed Virgin addressed to her cousin Elizabeth, Himana begged our Saint to tell her, what were her sentiments in meditating upon, or reciting this canticle. "That which I experience," said Juliana, in a sudden transport, and without reflecting upon what she said, "is so ineffable, that I would not change it for all the gold that this abbey could contain." The Abbess understood by this comparison that the joy and delight Juliana experienced in meditating upon the "Magnificat," were beyond all expression. No one was more reserved in her words, or more humble than Juliana; none more desirous of hiding the favours she received from God. Upon this occasion, however, Himana had asked this question when our Saint was seized with a sudden transport of love; so that she answered from the fulness of her heart and without reflection. When she perceived what she had done, she blushed at having been too prompt to reveal what ought to have been known to God alone, and she begged the abbess not to speak of that which she had revealed through her want of thought.

The graces and gifts God had bestowed formerly upon her, He still continued to favour her with, now that she was in exile. A religious of her acquaintance having been struck with a dangerous sickness, and there appearing no hope whatever of her recovery, Juliana asked and obtained from God, her entire restoration to health. The religious who was sick, lived at a considerable distance from the abbey; one of the sisters of the house, who also knew of the sickness of this religious, asked Juliana if she thought she would die; to which our Saint replied: "She is now out of danger, I shall die before her, and she will survive me, in order that she may be able to pray for me." They found, afterwards, upon inquiry, that the religious was out of danger, at the time Juliana had said; the prediction of Juliana was also verified, for the religious did survive our saint.

When she came from Namur to Salsines, they offered to conduct Juliana by water, on account of her age and infirmities; but she, foreseeing the accident that would occur to the boat, refused to be conveyed in this manner. She, therefore, together with her companion Isabella, went on foot, although it made the journey much longer. The boat which had been prepared for her, met with an accident, and sunk in a place where the waves of the Sambre had never before been agitated.

Juliana's life at Salsines had hitherto been calm and peaceful; but now it was God's good pleasure to try her, by taking from her the last of her companions, who had followed her from Cornillon. Isabella of Huy, her faithful companion, who had been a source of great comfort to our Saint in her many trials, was stricken with a mortal sickness, and died. The Abbess of Salsines, being anxious not to augment the grief of Juliana, caused the accustomed preparations for the funeral to be accomplished in such a manner, that Juliana should see little or nothing of them. But such precaution was not necessary; our saint was in this, as in all things else, perfectly resigned to the Holy Will of God. They interred Isabella near her former companions, Agnes and Ozila; but after the funeral the abbess visited our saint to console her, and found her in tears. The abbess, thinking that Juliana was grieving for the loss of her companion, reminded her that she ought not to weep, since Isabella, being so virtuous and holy a woman, had only exchanged this world for a better. To which Juliana replied, that her tears were tears of joy, because her dear friend had at length obtained the reward of her labours, virtues and devotion.

In all ordinary cases of the death of her friends and acquaintances, Juliana invariably prayed most fervently for them; but such was the high opinion she entertained of the holiness of Isabella, that she did not pray for her, because she believed her to be already in the possession of eternal beatitude, and consequently, no longer to stand in need of prayers. The abbess perceived that our saint did not pray for the repose of the soul of her friend, but said nothing until Isabella had been buried fifteen days. She then expressed to Juliana her astonishment that she offered no prayers for the repose of Isabella's soul. Our saint replied : " A very holy man once told me, that we do an injury to a saint by praying for him ; we ought rather to ask the saints to pray for *us*."

Juliana, having now no longer any of her sisters from Cornillon remaining with her, sent to Liège

12

for Ermentrude, a religious of great virtue; who obeyed her mother's commands, and came as soon as possible to Salsines. This holy religious is considered deserving of mention by the compiler of the Cistercian Menologium, in the following terms : " The blessed Ermentrude, nun of the Cistercian Order, died this day. She was instructed in the holy laws of our Institute at Mount Cornillon, near Liège ; she faithfully adhered to St. Juliana, and after many labours, departed in peace."* Ermentrude remained with Juliana until her death, faithfully ministering unto, and obeying her holy mother, who had taught her to walk in the paths of evangelical perfection.

Notwithstanding the many dissensions and disturbances that had taken place in the city of Liège, the most pious and devout of the citizens had always preserved a precious remembrance of our saint ; they could not easily forget her many virtues. Several of her former friends had even been to Salsines to see and console her. The late Prior of Cornillon, John, or to speak more correctly, the lawful Prior of Cornillon, also undertook this journey, in order, once more, to have the pleasure of seeing and conversing with her whom he so much respected. He met with a most gracious reception at Salsines, because his many virtues were not unknown to the abbess and her friends, for Juliana had lost no opportunities of eulogizing the virtues of one she so much respected. Before his return to Liège, she advised Ermentrude, her companion, to make her confession to him as to her legitimate pastor. " Do it," she said, " for in a short time neither you nor I will be able to do so, for he will no longer be living in this vale of tears." Her prophecy was

* Men. Cist. Apr. 7.

verified; for, very shortly after his return to Liège, he died the death of the just. The reader will remember that it was this holy man who composed the first Office of the Blessed Sacrament, in which both he and others recognized most visibly the finger of God. He is spoken of by the author of the Cistercian Menologium, in terms of the highest commendation: " At Liège died the Blessed John, Prior of Cornillon, of the Cistercian Order, a man of admirable piety and simplicity; who, through the exhortations of St. Juliana, composed the Office of the Venerable Sacrament not without miracle; (non sine miraculo,) and being adorned with great virtues, he departed to the celestial country."[*] The author then goes on to describe at greater length, the persecutions this man had to endure, and the many virtues and great sanctity he displayed during the course of his life. The most reliable authorities give the first of January, 1256, as the date of his death. Many authors have spoken in terms of the highest praise of this holy man, and we are assured that when they rebuilt the Church of Cornillon, his body was found perfect and entire, without any signs of corruption. The body was then placed in a vault, which was its last resting place.

Shortly after the departure of John for Liège, troubles arose at Salsines also, and reached their height about the time of his death; so that we suppose he never knew that Juliana had again to seek another asylum. The occasion of these new troubles was this. Mary, the niece of Queen Blanche, who was Countess of Namur, came to fix her residence near this city, and contracted a strong friendship with Himana, the Abbess of Salsines. One day that the countess visited the latter, in

---

* Men. Cist. Jan. 1.

the course of conversation the abbess told her that there was near the abbey a house of ill fame, where the master and several young gentlemen of dissolute manners like himself, abandoned themselves to all kinds of vices, and that it was a scandal to the whole district. In telling this to the countess, the abbess had no idea that she would have acted with so much precipitation, (not to say want of prudence,) as she did. She thought, indeed, that she would endeavour to remove the scandal; but she was not at all prepared for the energetic measures the countess took. No sooner did this lady learn from the lips of the abbess the scandal that was given by the house in question, than she ordered it to be razed to the ground, and her orders were immediately executed. The master of the house, enraged at this affront, entered with his accomplices into the city of Namur, and by their clamours excited the people to revolt. The governor, wishing to put an end to the riot, was killed by the mob; which irritated the countess so much, that she sought assistance from all sides to quell the riot, and succeeded at length in obtaining peace, at least, for the present.

The religious of Salsines congratulated themselves upon seeing peace restored, but not so Juliana; she was overwhelmed with sorrow because she saw the misfortunes which the religious of this abbey were soon to experience. The religious perceiving that she did not, as they, rejoice that this sad affair had terminated, wished to know the reason. Juliana answered: "This matter is not yet concluded, and when I consider the calamities which threaten the city of Namur, I should be the most ungrateful of women if I was not afflicted at the sight of so many persons of every state, condition, age, and sex, who will be reduced to the

greatest misery. We have received during our
exile too many marks of benevolence and charity,
not to mourn over their afflictions. But as the most
signal benefits have come to us from the Abbey
of Salsines, is it possible that its future desertion,
ruin, and solitude should not pierce my heart?
How can I see with a dry eye the affliction that
such disasters will cause the virtuous abbess to
experience, she who has not drawn upon herself
this chastisement? Would to God that she had
lived in other times! She has such good natural
dispositions, that if she had enjoyed peace, she
would have been elevated to a very intimate union
with God, and to the most sublime contemplation."

The evils that Juliana had foretold speedily
came to pass; those who had been engaged in the
riot, the master of the destroyed house and his
friends, leagued with the Count of Luxembourg,
and promised to assist him in his struggles to
obtain what he considered his rights over the
earldom of Namur. The Count of Luxembourg
armed secretly, and as promptly as he could;
advanced towards the capital, and entered on
Christmas night, 1256. During these troubles
the religious of Salsines were compelled to abandon their abbey, in order to escape the fury of the
dependants of Luxembourg. The abbess had,
without wishing or intending to do so, given
occasion for this war; if the house about which
she spoke had never been destroyed, the war
would never have happened. She deeply deplored
the disastrous consequences of the zeal of the
countess, and heartily wished that the latter had
endeavoured to extinguish vice in a milder manner.
Juliana was exceedingly afflicted at seeing her
kind friends and benefactors compelled to leave
their home. Himana wished to console her by

endeavouring to persuade her that the storm would soon pass over, and that they would soon return to their former home ; but Juliana predicted to the abbess that this hope would never be realised, and that she and her community would never return.   Our saint's prediction was verified to the letter.

The poor nuns were scattered about in divers places, and the abbess herself conducted Juliana and her companion Ermentrude, to Fosses, between Sambre and Meuse, where she procured them an asylum at the house of a canon of the collegiate church, who received them with joy, and endeavoured to console them as best he could. He was most happy to have an opportunity of conversing with Juliana, since he had heard much of the persecutions she had undergone, and of the great reputation for sanctity which she had acquired.

The sister of this canon had embraced the life of a recluse, and her brother had caused a cell to be built for her near the church ; but she, being now dead, the canon was thinking of having it pulled down.   The canon, however, seeing Juliana and her companion Ermentrude, in want of a home, offered them this cell.   Juliana was very grateful for the offer, and gladly accepted it; she was still more pleased when she found that the canon's deceased sister had embraced the state of a recluse upon the very day her friend Eva had conse-crated herself to the same holy manner of living at St. Martin's.   They therefore made all neces-sary preparations, and Juliana and her companion then took possession of it.   This was her last earthly home ; she had met with many troubles and changes ; she had suffered much persecution during her mortal pilgrimage, but her trials were now at an end, she was henceforth to pass her few remaining days in peace and quietness. Nothing was now to happen that could in any way disturb her close and intimate union with Him who was her One and only Treasure. She was now simply waiting for the dawn of that bright and glorious day which knoweth no evening, and whose sun shall no more go down. She was waiting to hear the voice of her Beloved calling her to Himself, and saying: "Arise, make haste, My love, My dove, My beautiful one, and come. For the winter is now past, the rain is over and gone. The flowers have appeared in our land, the time of pruning is come: the voice of the turtle is heard in our land: the fig-tree hath put forth her green figs: the vines in flower yield their sweet smell. Arise, My love, My beautiful one, and come."*

CHAPTER XV.

DEATH OF ST. JULIANA——THE HONOURS RENDERED TO HER AFTER HER DEATH.

THE peace, calmness, and tranquillity Juliana experienced in this little retreat, was a presage of approaching dissolution. It is true, her interior peace had never been disturbed, because she was too intimately united to God, for any earthly troubles (however great) to disturb her tranquillity. But now to this interior peace was joined exterior peace, she was no more to be troubled by any storms or tempests. She now began to experience here below a foretaste of that blissful, inexpressible

* Cant. ii. 10, 11, 12, 13.

peace which is the eternal portion of the blessed in heaven.

Not long after her entrance into this her last earthly home, she was attacked with her last sickness, if sickness it could be called ; for it seemed rather a languishing and pining away for Him who was the Supreme Object of all her desires. As she knew that death was the only remedy for the sickness with which she was stricken, she sent to Liège for John of Lausanne, canon of St. Martin's, whom she desired to see once more before she died. She inquired every day if there was any probability of his soon arriving. But whether he did not think her end so near, or that the siege of Namur rendered traveling in those quarters dangerous, or from some other cause, neither he nor any person from Liège came to see her.

She had a long time before said to one of her companions, that when her end approached, she should not have the happiness of seeing any of her old friends and confidants. Doubtless she had desired it, in order that she might communicate to them things that she had hidden all her life, even from her sisters. But as none of her old confidants arrived, if she had anything to declare, she had not the opportunity of declaring it ; her timidity forbidding her to declare it to any but to those who had during a long time enjoyed her confidence.

Her sickness proved to be rather a long one, but she bore all the pains and inconveniences of it with her accustomed courage, patience, and resignation. As she perceived her end approaching, she told Ermentrude that she should soon be taken from her ; but, at the first announcement of this news, Ermentrude burst into tears. Our saint endeavoured to console her as best she could, and reminded her that in all things we ought to resign ourselves to the 'adorable Will of God.

The bodily strength of the holy mother diminished daily, but her spiritual strength seemed to augment, according as she saw that moment approaching, in which she was to enjoy the glory of which she had already caught a glimpse, through the many and great graces God had bestowed upon her. She desired nothing more than to see her God for whom she had all her life so ardently longed, and therefore she constantly repeated the most ardent aspirations to her Beloved, begging of Him to bring her soul out of prison, that she might give thanks to His name. Her most frequent ejaculations were: "Lord, when shall You deliver me from this body of death?" "When shall You take me from this vale of tears?" "Lord, when shall I see You face to face?" Those who were present, and who heard her thus express her ardent desire to be with God, encouraged her, and told her that death was not far distant; but the word death was not pleasing to her, and she answered, "I shall not die, but live;" showing by these words that she looked upon death as the entrance into eternal life.

During the Lent her sickness grew worse; nevertheless, she continued to recite her Office, and by fervent and constant prayer to unite herself as closely as possible to God. When Easter Day arrived, all exhausted as she was, she prepared to go to the church. She assisted at Matins and Lauds without giving the least sign of fatigue. After these offices she received (from the hands of the canon of whom we have spoken above) the Holy Viaticum. Dying as she was, she nevertheless regarded herself as unworthy to have her Lord brought to her; and, therefore, although more than half dead, she forced herself to go to

the foot of the altar, in order to receive and adore
her Beloved.

With a most extraordinary courage, she, weak
as she was, remained the whole day in the church.
When she returned to her cell in the evening, she
requested that the Sacrament of Extreme Unction
should be administered to her. It was done as
she desired, and she received this sacrament with
great joy, pouring forth an abundance of tears, and
answering to the anointing of each member with
great fervour and recollection.

After receiving this Holy Sacrament, her one,
sole desire was to be united to God. Although it
was quite natural that she should feel the separation from her friends, and above all separation
from the Abbess of Salsines, who had been so
kind to her in her distress; nevertheless, the
love that she had for God, and the desire she had
to be united to Him, overcame this and every
other consideration. She ardently desired the
arrival of her last moment, not that she refused
to suffer again for her Beloved, if it was necessary;
but she knew the Lord now required no more of
her, and that it was His Will speedily to call her
to sing His praises for ever with the blessed in
heaven. Seeing then that her labours were over,
she desired to be delivered from this house of
bondage. She longed to behold Him Who had
always been the object of her love. Her soul
thirsted for God. She longed for the Fountain of
Life, the Spring of Living Waters. She ardently
desired to see God's beauty and glory, and quench
her thirst at the gushing streams of His love.
She had suffered trials and persecutions; she had
endured with heroic patience this life of exile,
which is the portion of all the banished children
of Eve; but now that she saw the approach of her
deliverance, she longed more and more for that

calm, glad, and thrilling life, which alone is true
life, in which we shall have nothing to fear from
our mortal and implacable enemy. For in that
kingdom of supreme, tranquil, and settled security,
the hateful enemy shall not enter, nor any breath
of temptation come near to hurt us. For this life
she longed; but, above all, she longed for Him
who in that kingdom of life and love, is the One,
Supreme Joy and Gladness of all His elect. Most
ardently did she desire to see face to face her God
and her All; the Joy of all joys; the Sweetness of
all sweetnesses; the Light of lights; the Love of
loves; the Life of all that lives.

The Abbess of Salsines, hearing of Juliana's
dangerous state, came to visit her; she was anxious to be present at the last moments of the holy
Prioress of Cornillon, and to see her pass into a
blessed eternity. It was Wednesday, and there
appearing every probability that the saint would
not live through the night, the abbess wished
to remain with Juliana all night, but she begged
the abbess to take some repose, assuring her that
she should not die that night. The abbess was
unwilling to retire, so certain did it appear that
Juliana's death would take place before morning;
but, upon our saint again assuring her that she
should not die that night, the abbess retired, feeling
confident that our saint was not deceived, and
thinking it most probable that God had Himself
revealed to her the day of her death. On the
Thursday she begged Ermentrude to recite the
Office aloud, and the holy mother followed her
with her heart, though too weak to do so with her
lips. On Friday the Abbess of Salsines visited
her early in the morning, accompanied with several
of her religious; as soon as they saw the holy
mother, they were convinced that her end was
near. The abbess asked Juliana if she would

like to adore her Saviour once more on earth ; her
infirmities did not permit her to receive the Holy
Communion, and therefore the abbess thought
that it would give her great pleasure once more
to adore Jesus in that sacrament of love, to which
she had always been so devout. Next to receiving
her Lord, nothing certainly could have given the
holy mother greater delight than to have the
opportunity of adoring Him really present under
the sacramental veils, but she thought herself
utterly unworthy of such a favour, so, when the
abbess asked her if she would like the Blessed
Sacrament to be brought, in order that for the
last time she might adore her Lord, Juliana
replied : " Ah ! it is not just that so great a Lord,
should visit so vile and worthless a creature."
The abbess, however, reminded her that it was
just that she should render to the Lord all the
homage and adoration of which she was capable.
Then Juliana begged, that all unworthy as she
was, her Lord might be brought to her.

Juliana who had, during the course of her life,
been an example of every virtue to all, was now
dying the death of the just. As she had given
much edification during her life, her death also was
to declare, how sweet it is for those to die, who
love God above all things, and who have sacrificed
all to belong to Him alone. As the time of her
dissolution drew near, her spiritual faculties and
perceptions seemed to become every moment clearer
and stronger. The aspirations which she breathed
forth to her Spouse were all burning with love ;
she had conversed with God all her life, but her
last moments seemed to be a recapitulation of all
the favours God had bestowed upon her during all
her mortal pilgrimage. At the time of her departure there was not the least signs of human
weakness or feebleness ; her eyes shone with su-

pernatural brightness; her cheeks were tinted with a beautiful vermilion; tears of ecstatic joy flowed from her eyes; she seemed to be already in the enjoyment of celestial beatitude.

When the priest brought the Blessed Sacrament, the moment she heard the sound of the bell, which announced to her the coming of her Lord, she cast herself upon her knees, and made most fervent acts of adoration and love. When the priest showed to her the Host, exhorting her to adore her Lord who was there really present, and telling her to beg of Him to conduct her safe to eternal rest, she said: "God be gracious to me and to this good abbess." These were the last words she spoke, and by them she declared, how grateful she was to the Abbess of Salsines for all her kindness. As she pronounced these few last words, she fixed her eyes upon the Host, and seemed to be conversing lovingly with her Lord, whom, with the eyes of faith, she saw beneath the sacramental veils; then, slightly inclining her head, in an ecstasy of love she passed away, on Friday, the 5th of April, 1258, in the sixty-sixth year of her age.*

Such was the death of this courageous heroine, who had suffered so much on the part of cruel and perverse men, whose conversion she never ceased to pray for. Her death was as holy as her life had been exemplary. Six different times she had been forced to leave the places she had chosen for her home. The victim of the persecutions of men who had determined to drive her far from her home; she died without having the consola-

---

* Chapeauville and some other authors give 1257 as the date of St. Juliana's death; but in 1257, the first Friday in April fell on the 6th and not on the 5th. Now it is beyond all contradiction, that Juliana died on the fifth of April, and on a Friday. Consequently, as in 1258 the 5th of April *did* fall on the Friday, 1258, and not 1257, is the real date of St. Juliana's death.

tion of being near to those who had through life been her dearest friends. Yet she never uttered one single word of complaint; no murmur passed her lips; she was perfectly and entirely resigned to all the misfortunes and persecutions God permitted her to experience. After the example of her Saviour, she prayed for her enemies, and was even willing to die for them, had this been necessary. Thus, as she had all her life clung to God and God alone, so at her last hour, having Him alone in view, she was rapt in an ecstasy of love; and in this manner she left this vale of tears to go and sing for ever the praises of Him, Who had always been the One and Only object of all her desires.

The Abbess of Salsines had desired that Juliana should be interred at her abbey, and had requested this favour from the holy mother some time before her death; but Juliana, who foresaw the ruin of this house, did not wish to be buried there. She therefore chose the Abbey of Villers, (a Cistercian abbey,) for the place of her sepulture. This abbey is situated on the confines of Brabant, about eighteen miles from Fosses. After the death of Juliana, a religious whose name was Gobert, and who was of the family of the Counts of Apremont, came to Fosses to take charge of her sepulture. Her funeral obsequies were in the meantime celebrated in the collegiate church of St. Feullian, at Fosses, after which the body of the holy mother was taken to the Abbey of Villers, upon a car prepared for the occasion. The Abbess Himana, Ermentrude, and several religious, accompanied the funeral procession out of veneration for the deceased, and after having performed these last duties of respect, they returned to Fosses.

The religious of Villers placed the body of St.

Juliana in the church ; according to custom, some of the religious kept up a continual prayer near the body of the holy mother, and on the next day they gave her a most honourable sepulture. It happened that upon this occasion, a priest who had not been invited to take part in the ceremony, came and delivered a most eloquent discourse upon the Blessed Sacrament. Thus, she who had all her life used every effort to spread devotion to this mystery of love, at her death also was the means of enkindling in the hearts of others, a greater devotion to the holy Sacrament of the Eucharist.

After her death people began to honour and invoke her as a saint, many had recourse to her intercession, and experienced speedily the effects of her power with God. This caused her to be still more honoured, hence there was a continual concourse of people who came to visit her tomb, and God, in order to show that this devotion to His servant was pleasing to Him, caused many miracles to be wrought at this holy shrine.

Henriquez, the Cistercian historian, speaking of the translation of the body of St. Juliana from Fosses to Villers, says, that they laid it behind the high altar, with the other relics of the abbey, and that it remained there for more than three centuries. During the troubles which agitated the Lower Countries, Robert Henrion, then Abbot of Villers, having built a magnificent chapel in honour of St. Bernard, caused the body of St. Juliana to be placed there, on the 17th of January, 1599. The body was laid in a tomb of black marble, very artistically wrought.

The decree of Pope Urban VIII., which forbids the title of Saint to those who have not been canonized by apostolic authority, has no reference whatever to our Saint Juliana; since it is expressly declared in this decree, that "it is not intended to prejudice those who have been honoured as saints by the common consent of the Church ; or from time immemorial, either by the writings of the fathers and holy men, or by the tolerance of the Holy See, or that of the Ordinary." " Non intellexit in aliquo præjudicare iis, qui per communem Ecclesiæ consensum, vel immemorabilem temporis cursum, aut per Patrum virorumque sanctorum scripta, vel longissimi temporis scientia ac tolerantia sedis Apostolicæ vel ordinarii coluntur." Now, St. Juliana died in the odour of sanctity, her body was placed amongst the relics of a celebrated abbey, a continual concourse of people visited her tomb and honoured her as a saint, many miracles were wrought through her intercession, she was universally recognised as a saint, and all this three hundred years before the constitution of Urban VIII. Therefore, according to the tenor of the decree, there is nothing to prohibit us from giving her the title of Saint.

Pope Innocent XII. calls her Saint in his bull of the 27th of February, 1696, on the occasion of the indulgence he granted to those of both sexes who visited the church of Cornillon on the day of the Feast. Benedict XIII. gives her the same title, in a bull for the erection of a confraternity in honour of St. Juliana. A Mass for her Feast is inserted in many Missals, and a Plenary Indulgence is granted on her Feast to the Cistercians of the Congregation of La Trappe, by the present holy and venerable Pontiff Pius IX. Her Feast also, is now celebrated by the Cistercians.

All ecclesiastical historians unanimously speak of her as a saint, universally recognised as such. Ferrarius, Blærus, Wion, Saussaye, Miræus, Bernard de Brito, Mauriquez, Henriquez, Chapeauville, Molanus, Bzovius, Haribert Roswedus,

Oderic Reynaldus, Fannius, Fisen, and many others, all give her the title of saint.

The Apology for the canonization of Juliana, given by the Bollandists in the Acta Sanctorum, April. tom. I., is so conclusive that we take the liberty of translating it, and giving it here in English.

"Lest any one should say that Juliana has become celebrated in the Church only on account of the revelation she had concerning the Institution of the Feast of Corpus Christi, and that she was not anciently honoured as a saint, we will briefly collect here the different proofs of the honours which have been rendered to her. In the first place, it is evident from ancient histories, that by the unanimous consent of the clergy and people, the title of Saint, or Blessed, has always been given to her; there is also at Retine, the village of her birth, a fountain which is still called 'the fountain of St. Juliana.' In the second place, her solemn sepulture amongst the holy bodies of the Abbey of Villers, is well known to all; they would never have interred her in this manner if they had not esteemed her as a saint, since she was an exiled virgin, poor, and without any recommendation than that which the good odour of her virtues could give. They erected to her a monument of marble four feet high, to which was appended a prayer common to the saints whose relics the church contained, but proper to Juliana. They have, moreover, inserted her name in the litany used at the Abbey of Floreffe, where she is invoked in this manner: 'Blessed Juliana, illuminated by many revelations from heaven; whom God hath chosen as an instrument to promote the annual celebration of the Feast of Corpus Christi through the whole Church, on which account thy praise is exceeding great; pray for us.'

13

"Another argument for the canonization of Juliana is drawn from four statues, which have all the indications usually attributed to the saints. The first is of wood, placed near the pillar of the choir of the church of Cornillon, opposite one of St. Austin, of similar workmanship. It is a very ancient statue, and has been there from time immemorial; on account of its age, it was necessary to have it repainted. Formerly the head was surrounded with flowers, but latterly they have substituted a crown. This statue is, and was from time immemorial, exposed for public veneration. The people were accustomed to pray before it, and to burn lights; moreover, the Burgomasters of Liège, upon the Feast of St. Augustine, the patron of the church, honoured this statue of St. Juliana, in the same manner as that of St. Augustine, by an offering of a bouquet of flowers.

"The second statue, of similar form, exists in the parish church of Fleron, where it is every year carried in procession before the Blessed Sacrament, in memory of the revelation which Juliana had concerning the Institution of this Feast, and to honour the village of Retine, the place of Juliana's birth, which depends on this parish. The third is of stone, in the church of Cornillon, near the tabernacle, and now nearly effaced by age; it is similar in form to the other two, and exhibits the name of St. Juliana. The fourth, which was on the silver monstrance of the same church, answered to the figure of an angel on the opposite side, having the head surrounded with rays, and the hands extended, as it were to sustain the Blessed Sacrament. Although they have changed the form of this monstrance, and have remodelled it, nevertheless, there are ocular witnesses of this fact, and among others the workman who remodelled it, the Prior of the

Carthusians, and his religious. To perpetuate the memory of the former, they have added to the new work a double image of Juliana: the first representing the vision of the moon, obscured by one dark spot; the other representing the apparition of the holy Apostles Peter and Paul.

"The other proofs that antiquity furnishes for the canonization of St. Juliana, are drawn from her images and pictures, engraved, printed, and distributed among the people, all of which have some indications of her sanctity. The most ancient of all represents the Blessed Sacrament, sustained by the hands of Juliana, (whose head is surrounded with rays of light,) and Isabella; but adored by St. Augustine and Eva the recluse. Another more recent one represents only the figures of Juliana, Isabella, and Eva, adoring the Blessed Sacrament; but Juliana, who is in the midst, alone hath the head surrounded with a diadem, or luminous circle. This is dedicated to the dean and canons of the collegiate church of St. Martin, and is painted on the altar of the chapel of the Confraternity of the Blessed Sacrament, established in this church. Copies of it are annually distributed among the members of the Confraternity. A third, indeed, representing Juliana alone, adoring the Blessed Sacrament, and having a diadem upon her head, is in the church of Cornillon, and copies of it are every year distributed amongst the members of the Confraternity of St. Juliana, and others who are devout to this saint. Again, the walls of the church of Mount Cornillon have from time immemorial been adorned with large pictures representing the different periods of the life of St. Juliana, which, being consumed by age, have been renewed three different times; but they have always substituted others of the same design as the old ones. On the principal wall of the church there is a picture of St. Juliana in ecstasy, and having the head surrounded with rays of light. Also in the church of Villers there is a picture of St. Juliana and of the other saints whose relics this church contains, and the title of Blessed is written beneath."

Juliana was honoured as a saint, not only at Liège and in the surrounding countries, but also in the kingdom of Portugal ; Margaret of Parma, returning into Italy, took some of our saint's relics to Rome, (this was in the 16th century,) from whence the King of Portugal took some of them for his private chapel. These same relics were afterwards sent to the monastery of St. Saviour at Anvers, belonging to the Cistercian Order, and the translation of these relics was celebrated on the 7th of August, 1672.

After the death of Juliana, the people of Liège, who knew well the virtues of Juliana, and the persecutions she had so patiently endured, began to honour her as a saint. We may well believe that she who during life had obtained many favours from God, for so many of the inhabitants of this city and diocese, would obtain for them still more, now that she was in the enjoyment of the Beatific Vision, and that this people were now asking the help of her powerful prayers. That many favours were obtained by the people of Liège, through the intercession of St. Juliana, is evidenced by the great increase of the devotion of this people to our saint, which became so great, that the Office of St. Juliana was inserted in the Breviary of the diocese of Liège, and they celebrate her Feast with an octave on the 5th of April, in the church of Cornillon, where there is a confraternity in her honour. We know that many miracles were wrought at her tomb, and that abundance of graces and blessings were obtained through her intercession in various places, and we cannot believe that she did not obtain many favours for that city and diocese, where the Feast that she laboured and suffered so much to promote was first celebrated. If she had met with opposition and persecution from some of the people, be it remembered that it was not from the good that she had experienced this; but from the wicked, the depraved, and those who were lost to every sense of honour, and who gloried in their vices and wickedness. The good had always respected her, and sincerely endeavoured to imitate her virtues; but she happened to live in times of disorder, agitation, and confusion, and so the few who were her enemies had ample opportunities of persecuting her. But, doubtless, the fervent prayers she offered to God for her persecutors, obtained for many of them the grace of an entire, true, and sincere conversion. At least let us hope so.

Our saint now enjoys the blissful presence of God, she beholds Him face to face. Let us therefore ask her to pray for us, and obtain for us a portion of that great love and devotion to the Sacrament of the Eucharist, which she had when here below. Let us implore her to obtain for ourselves, and for others, and above all, for those who know not the truth; faith, love, and devotion for the Sacrament of the Altar, that prodigy of love, that divine institution, wherein Christ Himself, our most benign Jesus, is at once the banquet and the guest, the offering and the offerer, our food and refreshment, our nourishment and our life. For, " being a merciful and gracious Lord, He hath given food to them that fear Him."*

* Psalm cx. 4, 5.

CHAPTER XVI.

CONCLUSION.

The Institution of the Feast of Corpus Christi, having necessarily been so much spoken of in the life of St. Juliana, and she having had so intimate a connection with, and having been so ardent a promoter of it; in order to render our subject more complete we shall now, in conclusion, briefly relate the history of its institution throughout the entire Church. For, since our saint suffered so much in promoting this good work, the reader will doubtless be delighted to see in how wonderful a manner the prediction of St. Juliana was verified. It will be remembered that our saint foretold that this Feast would be celebrated throughout the entire Church, to the great delight and joy of the faithful. We shall now see how all this came about.

We have said in a previous chapter, that after the departure of the legates of the Holy See, Hugh of St. Cher, and Peter Capoche, their decrees relative to the Feast of Corpus Christi were no longer respected, and that even a contradictory decree had been published by some ecclesiastics. But the friends of St. Juliana, and, above all, Eva the recluse of St. Martin's, had never ceased to do all they could to promote the celebration of the new Feast. Some time before the death of Juliana, the city and diocese of Liège had well nigh returned to its former state of peace and quietness, and after her death, many, hearing of the holy end of the Prioress of Cornillon, and the wonders that had been wrought through her powerful intercession, returned from their former prejudices, and began to believe that the Feast she had striven so much to promote, would be for the greater honour and glory of God, and the benefit of all the faithful.

So much had the prejudices of the opponents of the Feast given way, that by the time of the election of Urban IV. to the dignity of Sovereign Pontiff, (which took place on the 29th of August, 1261,) Eva thought it was quite time to solicit the confirmation of the institution of the new Feast from the Holy See. The accession of Urban IV. to the Papal throne seemed to her a favourable opportunity for obtaining this favour, since the new Pope was well known to be a zealous promoter of everything calculated to give honour and glory to God.

The recluse, therefore, communicated her thoughts to the canons of St. Martin's, and begged them to persuade the bishop to ask from the Pope, the confirmation of the Institution of the Feast of Corpus Christi. The canons, who had always been strenuous promoters of the Feast, were only too happy to comply with Eva's request. They therefore spoke of this matter to the bishop, who listened favourably to them. He was anxious to gain the friendship and esteem of all his clergy, and as he knew the most virtuous and learned amongst them desired to see this Feast celebrated throughout the whole diocese, he most willingly listened to the representations of the canons of St. Martin's; knowing that by so doing, he should gain the esteem of those amongst his clergy whose friendship he valued. Henry of Gueldre, therefore, wrote to the Pope to congratulate him upon his elevation to the Papal See, and at the same time begged His Holiness to confirm the decrees of Bishop Robert, and the Cardinals Hugh of St. Cher and Peter Capoche, relative to the celebration of the Feast of Corpus Christi.

The zeal of Urban IV. for everything calculated to give honour and glory to God, caused him to accede most willingly to the request of Henry of Gueldre, the Bishop of Liège. He approved of the decrees of Bishop Robert and the Cardinals, and gave his sanction for the celebration of the Feast, in the Diocese of Liège. Then the ecclesiastics and others, who had formerly opposed the celebration of the Feast, now that they saw the Sovereign Pontiff approve the design, withdrew their opposition, and celebrated it. The canons of St. Martin's alone have the honour of having been all the time obedient to the decrees of Bishop Robert and the Cardinals, for they alone of the whole diocese of Liège regularly celebrated the Feast upon the day appointed. But in the year 1262, the Feast was, according to the will and desire of the Pope, celebrated in all the churches of the diocese of Liège.

The new Feast having thus been established and celebrated in the Diocese of Liège, it was soon found that its celebration in one diocese only would not satisfy the devotion of the people. The many benefits and graces which the celebration of the new Feast brought along with it, caused devotion to it to spread far and wide. Moreover, several wonderful things having happened in connection with the celebration of the Feast, and these things having been witnessed by persons well known for their probity and learning, as well as by their dignity, it was not long before the faithful desired to have this Feast celebrated by the entire Church.

The Holy Father Urban IV., who had a great devotion to the Sacrament of the Eucharist, seeing that so many desired the Feast to be established throughout Christendom, believed that the time had come for him to publish the Bull for its institution. In order that the rite should be everywhere the same, he confided the composition of a new Office to St. Thomas of Aquin, who was at this time at Orvieto. When the saint had accomplished the task assigned to him, the Sovereign Pontiff examined the work, and found it so beautiful and so full of unction, that he sent copies of it to all the churches in Christendom together with his Bull for the institution of the Feast. The Bull of the Holy Father is as follows :

" Urban, bishop, servant of the servants of God, to our venerable Brethren, the Patriarchs, Archbishops, Bishops and other Prelates of the Church. When our Lord and Saviour Jesus Christ was about to leave this world and return to His Father, He, the night before His Passion, after having eaten the Paschal Lamb with His disciples, instituted the most holy Sacrament of His Body and Blood, giving Himself to us for our food and nourishment; for as often as we eat this bread and drink of this chalice, we show forth the death of the Lord. When instituting this mystery, He said to His apostles, ' Do this in remembrance of Me,' desiring to make known to us by these words that the great and venerable Sacrament He had just instituted, was the great and signal memorial of the infinite love, wherewith He hath loved us ; an admirable and striking memorial, agreeable, sweet, and more precious than all things ; where signs and wonders are wrought, where we find all sweetness and delight, and from whence we can draw an assured pledge of eternal life.

"It is the most sweet memorial, the sacred and salutary memorial, which recalls to our minds the happy moment of our Redemption, which draws us from evil, which strengthens us in good, which produces in us an increase of virtue and grace; in fine, which conducts us safely in the path to heaven. The other mysteries that the Church celebrates, we adore in spirit and truth; but in the Sacrament of the Eucharist, Jesus Christ is really present, and there dwells truly with us. When He ascended to heaven, He said to His disciples: 'Lo I am with you always, even to the consummation of the world,' thus encouraging them and assuring them that He should always remain with them by His corporal presence.

"O most worthy and ever venerable memorial, which reminds us that death hath no sting, that we are no longer lost, since the vivifying Body of the Lord, which was nailed to the tree of the Cross, hath restored us to life! This is that glorious memorial which fills the faithful with a salutary joy, and which causes them to shed tears of love and gratitude. At the remembrance of our Redemption we triumph; and in calling to our minds the death of Jesus Christ Who has redeemed us, we cannot refrain from weeping. This sacred memorial of the death of Christ, therefore, procures us both joy and tears; we rejoice in weeping, and we weep in rejoicing; because our hearts being overwhelmed with delights, by the memory of so great a gift, we cannot refrain from shedding tears of gratitude.

"O abyss of Divine love! O superabundance of the mercy of our God! O astounding marvel of His liberality! Not content with having appointed us masters of the goods of earth, He has also submitted all creatures to us, and hath given us dominion over them. Nor did He stop here;

He esteemèd the dignity of man so elevated, that He gave him an angel for a guardian, since the celestial spirits minister unto us, and conduct the predestined to the possession of that inheritance which is prepared for them in heaven. And after such shining testimonies of His magnificence, He has been pleased also to give us other proofs of His inexpressible charity, by giving us Himself, and exceeding the plenitude of every gift, and every measure of love, He hath given Himself to be our food and nourishment.

" O eminent and admirable liberality, where the Giver passes into the Gift, where the thing given is the same as Him Who gives it ! O prodigality unparalleled, where the Giver gives Himself! Our God has therefore given Himself to be our food, because man, condemned to death, can only return to life by this means. He died in eating of the forbidden fruit, and he lives by tasting of the Tree of Life. The eating of the former gave a wound, the tasting of the latter restored to health ; the former taste has wounded, and the latter has healed. For He said of the former : ' In the day you eat of it you shall die ;' but of the latter, He said : ' Whosoever eateth of this bread shall live for ever.'

" O substantial meat, which fully satisfies, which truly nourishes, and which sovereignly feeds, not the body, but the heart ; not the flesh, but the soul ; not the belly, but the spirit ! Our merciful Saviour, by a tender and charitable love, seeing that man stood in need of a spiritual aliment, has therefore provided for the soul the most noble and efficacious food. It was by a most beneficent liberality, and by a most tender and agreeable goodness, that the Eternal Word of God, Who is the food and refreshment of His creatures, being made flesh, hath given Himself to flesh; I mean to say, to man for food. For, 'Man hath eaten the Bread of Angels,' and therefore our Lord hath said : ' My flesh is meat indeed.' This Divine bread is eaten, but it is not changed, because it is not transformed into him who eats it; but he who eateth it, if he eateth worthily, is transformed into Him Whom he receives.

" O excellent, adorable, venerable Sacrament, which we ought to honour and glorify, which we can never extol and exalt according to its merits! O Sacrament, worthy of being revered with the whole extent of our hearts, worthy of being loved with the greatest affection and tenderness, worthy of being so profoundly engraven upon our souls, as that it could never be effaced! O most noble memorial, which we ought to declare, extol and exalt in every place, which all Christians should call to their remembrance with the most lively gratitude, which should be impressed on our souls, and which we can never sufficiently meditate upon nor celebrate too piously! We are, therefore, obliged to preserve a continual remembrance of it, in order that we may continually have Him before our eyes, whose inestimable benefits it represents to us; for the more frequently we consider the presents we have received, the more we are attached to the person who has given them to us.

" But, although we daily commemorate this mystery in the Sacrifice of the Mass, we nevertheless believe that it is very meet and right, in order to confound the foolishness of heretics, that we should, at least once a year, celebrate a more special and more solemn Feast in honour of this Sacrament. Maundy Thursday, the day on which Jesus Christ instituted this Sacrament, being taken up with the reconciliation of sinners, the washing of the feet, and other mysteries, we cannot give ourselves up entirely to the celebration of this august Sacrament; this is the reason it is proper to assign another day for this. For the rest, this is the practice of the Church in regard of the saints, who notwithstanding that they are daily invoked, by prayers, in the Litanies, in the Mass, and on other occasions, have also proper days in the course of the year, on which they are more especially honoured.

"Moreover, as upon these Feast days the people do not always fulfil their religious duties, whether by negligence, or on account of domestic occupations, or it may be through human feebleness; on which account our holy mother the Church has appointed a certain day on which all saints are generally commemorated, in order, that in this solemnity the omissions which have happened in the other Feasts should be repaired. But if such is the custom of the Church, how much more reason have we to practise it in regard to the vivifying Sacrament of the Body and Blood of Jesus Christ, Who is the glory and the crown of all saints. We shall thus have the advantage of supplying by a pious diligence, for all the faults we may have committed at the Masses we have offered up or assisted at during the course of the year. Moreover, the faithful, at the approach of this Feast, calling to mind their past faults, will come in all humility and purity of heart to expiate them, and to ask of God pardon for the irreverences committed during the time of Mass, or for their negligence in assisting at it.

"When, heretofore, we were constituted in lesser dignity in the Church, we learned that it had been Divinely revealed to certain Catholics, that the Feast of Corpus Christi should be solemnized throughout the universal Church. We, therefore, in order to fortify and exalt the Orthodox Faith, have thought proper to ordain, that besides the daily commemoration which the Church makes of this Divine Sacrament, there shall be celebrated every year a solemn Feast in its honour ; we name a day expressly for this purpose, to wit, the Thursday after the Octave of Pentecost. Upon which day the devout multitude shall visit our churches, where the clergy, as well as the laity, filled with holy joy, shall sing canticles of praise. Therefore, upon this holy day, let the faithful with heart and voice sing hymns of joy ; upon this memorable day let faith triumph, hope increase, charity burn ; let the pious rejoice, let our temples resound with melodious chants, and pure souls leap with joy. Upon this day of devotion let all the faithful run with joy of heart and prompt obedience, to acquit themselves of their duties, in order that they may worthily celebrate so great a Feast. May it please God so to inflame their hearts, that by their pious exercises they may increase in merit before Him Who hath given Himself as the price of their redemption, and may He Who presents Himself to be their nourishment in this life, be their recompense in the life to come.

" Therefore we entreat and exhort you in our Lord, and by this Apostolic constitution we command you, by virtue of holy obedience, and we enjoin you, in order to obtain remission of your sins, that you every year devoutly celebrate upon the aforesaid day, this excellent and glorious Feast, and that you cause it to be celebrated in all the churches of your dioceses. Moreover, we ordain you to exhort your subjects, by yourselves and by others, upon the Sunday preceding the Feast, that they so prepare themselves by an entire and sincere confession, by alms, by prayers and by other good works, that they may deserve upon this day to be partakers of this most precious Sacrament, that they may receive it with respect, and by this means obtain an increase of grace.

"As we desire to animate the faithful by spiritual gifts to celebrate and respect this Feast, we grant one hundred days indulgence to all those who, being truly contrite, shall have confessed their sins, and shall assist upon this day at Matins, or Mass, or First Vespers; and to those who assist at Prime, Tierce, Sext, None or Compline, forty days indulgence for each of these hours. Moreover, to all those who, during the Octave, shall assist at Matins, Vespers and Mass, we, supporting ourselves on the merciful power of God, and confiding in the authority of the blessed Apostles Peter and Paul, grant each time one hundred days indulgence."

Pope Urban IV. gives himself, in this Bull, the reasons which induced him to institute the Feast, in these words : "When, heretofore, we were constituted in lesser dignity in the Church, we learned that it had been Divinely revealed," &c. So that before he ascended the Papal throne, he had been acquainted with, and approved of, the vision of Juliana relative to the institution of the Feast of Corpus Christi. To our saint then, must we, under God, acknowledge ourselves indebted for the institution of this glorious Feast.

The Pope employed all his care and authority to cause the Feast to be universally received in the Church. Some ecclesiastics of the Diocese of Liège being at this time in Rome, the Pope, who knew that our saint had been the most zealous promoter of the new Feast, inquired of them if she still lived. They answered no; but that her faithful friend Eva still lived, and that she had inherited many of the virtues of Juliana, and, in particular, her zeal for the promotion of the new Feast. The Pope, upon hearing this, believed he should reanimate Eva's piety and devotion, if he congratulated her upon the success of the work she had so much at heart. He, therefore, not long afterwards, addressed to her the following brief:

"Urban, bishop, to our dear daughter in Jesus Christ, Eva, recluse of St. Martin's, at Liège, health and benediction. We know, my dear daughter, that with your whole soul you have desired, that the solemn Feast of the most sacred Body of our Lord Jesus Christ should be instituted in the Church of God. We therefore announce to you joyful tidings, and we signify to you that in order to establish more and more firmly the Catholic Faith, we have thought proper to ordain, that besides the daily commemoration that the Church makes of this adorable Sacrament, a special Feast should be celebrated, for which purpose we have appointed a day, upon which the faithful may devoutly frequent our churches; a day which shall become for all a Feast of great joy, as we have more amply expressed in our letters.

"Furthermore, we wish you to know, that we ourselves, in order to give to the Christian world a salutary example of this solemnity, have celebrated this Feast in presence of the Archbishops, Bishops and other Prelates of the Church, who reside near our Apostolic See. Therefore, let your soul magnify the Lord; let your spirit rejoice in Him, because your eyes have seen the great and good things which are prepared before the face of all people. Rejoice, because the Omnipotent God hath granted you the accomplishment of your desires; and may the plenitude of celestial grace put in your mouth canticles of praise and jubilation.

"As we send to you, by the bearer of our present letters, our Bull, and also a copy of the Office for the Feast of Corpus Christi, we will and we ordain you by this brief, to receive it with devotion, and to deliver a copy of it to all persons who shall request it. We also request you to pray most fervently to Him Who has left upon earth such an august memorial of Himself, that He may grant us grace from on high to govern usefully the holy Church, which He has confided to our care.

"Given at Orvieto, the eighth day of September, in the fourth year of our Pontificate."

We can better imagine than describe, the joy the holy recluse felt in receiving this brief. She now saw the predictions of her friend and mother, the Blessed Juliana, fulfilled to the letter. She saw that Feast which she had desired so ardently to be celebrated, not merely approved and confirmed, but extended to all the Church, by the authority of Christ's vicar on earth. She could now say with holy Simeon: "Lord, now Thou dost dismiss Thy servant in peace," and indeed, shortly after this, she gave up her soul to God, and left this troublesome world for the land of everlasting peace. She is mentioned in the Cistercian Menologium, and is there called Blessed. Several other authors also give her the same title. In the Church of St. Martin, at Liège, there is a wooden statue representing Eva holding in her left hand the Apostolic Brief of Urban IV. Below the statue is the inscription: "Beata Eva, Ora pro nobis."

The original of the brief which Urban IV. sent to Eva was preserved in the archives of the collegiate church of St. Martin, but, unhappily, it was consumed in the fire which happened during

14

some disturbances in the city of Liège. Fortunately, however, many copies of it still exist, so that this precious monument has not been lost to posterity.

Urban IV. died on the 2nd of October, 1264, about one month after sending his brief to Eva; but what he had instituted was confirmed by Clement V., and after him by John XXII. This last ordained the Feast of Corpus Christi to be celebrated with an octave, and that the Blessed Sacrament should be carried in procession through the streets and public places. Martin V., Eugene IV., and other Pontiffs, have since confirmed the decrees of their predecessors, and added new indulgences.

Thus was this glorious Feast instituted in the Church of God, and is now celebrated throughout the Christian world with great joy and gladness. The prediction of St. Juliana we see realised, as each year brings round this gladdening solemnity. And as from the heaven where now she dwells, she looks down upon this lower world and sees with what joy the faithful celebrate this Feast, and what honour and glory is thereby given to God, surely, by the accidental glory that this procures her, she is more than recompensed for all the trials, troubles, and persecutions she endured in endeavouring to procure its celebration. She is now receiving the reward of her love and devotion; she loved her Lord when on earth; she adored Him and worshipped Him with her whole heart, when in this vale of tears she saw Him with the eyes of faith beneath the sacramental veils; but now she is rewarded for this devotion by seeing face to face, Him whom in this life she adored by faith. Now she no longer sees Him through a glass in a dark manner, but she sees Him as He is. She spared neither pains nor labour to enkindle in the hearts of others devotion to this Sweet Sacrament of love, and she is now being refreshed after her toils with the waters of Life which flow from the Saviour's fountains. If, in doing what she could to promote God's honour and glory, she met with persecution, she now experiences the sweetest consolation. On earth she sowed in tears, but now she is gathering the fruits with joy and gladness. It is impossible for us to say, how many souls have been brought to God, by the celebration of that Feast she laboured so much to promote, certainly we know that it is never celebrated without many sinners being reconciled to God. Now, if there is joy in heaven over one sinner that repenteth, what must be the joy of our saint when she sees that through her labours, toils, and sufferings, so many are reconciled to God, who, had it not been for the occasion of reconciliation which this Feast presents, would probably never have been reconciled to Him at all ? Ah, it is impossible for us either to think or conceive, the torrent of delights which inundate her soul as each sinner is thus brought to God. She might have refused to undertake this work, but she did not, and because she corresponded to the grace of God, and hearkened to His voice, which called her to cooperate with Him in this work ; He now hath rewarded her by bestowing upon her a happiness, a bliss, a joy, which is so ecstatic, so enrapturing, so beatific, as to surpass all speech or thought.

Let us then, as far as possible, imitate St. Juliana in her devotion to this stupendous mystery. Almighty God may not require of us to undergo as many labours and trials as she bore, but at least let us manifest as much reverence and love to this mystery of love, as we poor, weak mortals are capable of. There are many ways by which we can show to Jesus that we are grateful for this gift, by reverential behaviour and comportment in His presence; by visiting Him as often as our occupations will permit; by frequently receiving Him with all possible devotion and fervour; by celebrating the Feast of this sweetest Sacrament of Jesus' love with piety and deepest reverence; by joining confraternities which are now, in almost every parish, established in honour of this Sacrament; in fine, there are a variety of ways by which we can prove to our Lord that we are really grateful and thankful for this unspeakable, inestimable gift.

Surely it is meet, right, just, and salutary that we should show ourselves grateful for this priceless treasure, for in this Sacrament Jesus hath poured forth all the riches of His divine love for man. In this Sacrament the most astounding prodigies are gathered together, and it contains the profound mysteries of God. This Divine Sacrament possesses, by concomitance, and ever recalls to the minds of the faithful, the sublimest of mysteries, the mystery of the Most Holy Trinity. In this thrice Blessed Sacrament is also contained and extended in a marvellous manner, the mystery of the Incarnation. For here the same Jesus, God and Man, who by the Incarnation dwelt in the womb of the ever Blessed Virgin, dwells by Holy Communion in the hearts of all who devoutly receive Him. Here in this mystery of love is the Bethlehem where faithful souls find Jesus more speedily and more easily, than the shepherds and the Magi found Him in the stable. Here is the sanctuary wherein Jesus is presented to God the Father, and devoted to the salvation of men. Here is the temple where He is occupied about His Father's business. Here is Nazareth where He leads a hidden and obscure life.

In this venerable sacrament we find Jesus our Saviour, who came to seek and to save them that were lost, and who gives to every poor thirsty soul that approaches, the living water that springeth up unto life everlasting. Here is the Good Shepherd who feedeth His flock with His own most Sacred Body. Here is the Light that enlighteneth every man that cometh into the world. Here is the kind Father, who tenderly embraces His prodigal son the moment he returns to his loving Father's arms. Here is the Physician who heals every wound, alleviates every pain. Here is the Teacher who by His secret whisperings teaches us the mysteries of His love. Here is the Bridegroom of virginal and chaste souls, whom He espouses to Himself, and who follow Him whithersoever He goeth. Here is Heaven on earth; here is Jesus, our God and our All.

O prodigy of love! O abyss of marvels! O admirable Sacrament! O priceless treasure! O sweeter than all sweetest delights! O mystery of mysteries! O Sacrament of love! O Love Divine! Would, O God of Love, that we could praise and bless Thee for this gift transcending all gifts, as Thou deservest! but neither men nor angels are capable of rendering to Thee the thanks that are due. As far as creatures can praise Thee, may never-ending praise be given to Thee, for the institution of this Sacrament of love. Come, all ye tribes and people of the earth, and give ye thanks to the Lord, for He is good and His mercy endureth for ever. O ye angels, ministers and messengers of the Most High, declare ye everywhere the wonders of Jesus' love for man. Come ye Cherubim, and with your marvellous intelligences contemplate this mystery of love, and, piercing beneath the sacramental veils, adore with profoundest adoration your Lord and God, who is hidden there. Come ye Seraphim, all burning with love, adore and love our Jesus for us. O peerless, spotless Virgin, Immaculate Mother of this same Jesus Christ our Lord and God, whom we receive in this Sacrament, do thou praise and bless and thank Him for us, who are incapable of doing it ourselves; thy thanks, O Blessed Lady, He will accept, for thou art full of grace, thou art pure, and there is no stain of original sin in thee; the praises and thanksgivings of thy Pure Heart will be acceptable to Him. Do thou, Immaculate Virgin, by thy powerful intercession, obtain that this Sacrament of love may be known and reverenced by all the nations upon earth. O God, be Thou blessed for this Thy great gift to man. "May the name of Thy Majesty be blessed for ever, and may the whole earth be filled with the praise of Thy name. Fiat. Fiat. Amen. Amen."

PRINTED BY RICHARDSON AND SON, DERBY.

CPSIA information can be obtained
at www.ICGtesting.com
Printed in the USA
BVHW04s1945090818
524066BV00015B/100/P